The Gift of Sleep

The Gift of Sleep

Elizabeth Sloane

ALLEN&UNWIN

SYDNEY · MELBOURNE · AUCKLAND · LONDON

First published in 2017

Originally published as an ebook in 2013 by Mamamia Publishing.
Excerpt on pages 29–31, 66, 83 and 112 reprinted with the kind permission of the
Murdoch Childrens Research Institute.

Allen & Unwin
83 Alexander Street
Crows Nest NSW 2065
Australia
Phone: (61 2) 8425 0100
Email: info@allenandunwin.com
Web: www.allenandunwin.com

Cataloguing-in-Publication details are available
from the National Library of Australia
www.trove.nla.gov.au

ISBN 978 1 76029 6780

Index by Puddingburn
Set in 13.1/18 pt Garamond Premier Pro by Bookhouse, Sydney
Printed and bound in Australia by Griffin Press

10 9 8 7 6 5 4 3 2 1

For every parent who
has ever walked the halls
despairing at 2 a.m.

Contents

About the author   ix
A note from the author   xi
Foreword by Mia Freedman   1

Chapter 1 Who is Elizabeth Sloane?   17
Chapter 2 The case for and against controlled crying   25
Chapter 3 What is the Gift of Sleep program and is it right
    for my baby?   33
Chapter 4 The nine Golden Rules   41
Chapter 5 The Gift of Sleep program   47
  Preparing the nursery   49
  The three Cs   55
  Beginning the Gift of Sleep program   57
  Program for babies aged six to eleven months   61
  Program for babies aged twelve to eighteen months   75
  Program for children aged eighteen months to five
      years old   93
  Twins   100
  Premature babies   101
Chapter 6 Frequently asked questions   103
Chapter 7 Dos and don'ts for the next 30 days   125
Chapter 8 Case Studies   129
Chapter 9 How to not need this book with your next child   139

Reference guide   147
Testimonials   163
Worksheets   179
So now what?   195
Acknowledgements   197
Index   199

About the Author

Elizabeth Sloane has been giving babies the gift of sleep for over 20 years. With a gentle, loving and soothing nature, Elizabeth's methods are credited with breaking cycles of sleeplessness, emotional exhaustion and frustration for babies and their parents—a truly life-changing experience. Her program offers a calm, committed and consistent approach to all families in need of the Gift of Sleep.

Elizabeth had always enjoyed looking after young babies and children but felt like there was little support for parents with babies over six months old with sleep issues. Following her heart, she discovered a unique talent in teaching babies and toddlers to self-settle and soon found herself inundated with requests for help. Having honed her craft over the past two decades, Elizabeth is deeply committed to each family, ensuring that their baby reaches their goal. She lives in Sydney with her beautiful family.

A note from the author

Before you start any sleep program, I recommend you go to your paediatrician, child health nurse or GP and get the tick of approval that your baby is 100 per cent healthy. It's also important to know that crying is a normal part of a baby's existence. After all, it's how they communicate with us! My Gift of Sleep program is not about stopping babies from crying—not at all. Instead, it is a program specifically designed to lovingly correct those unhealthy sleep habits your child may have developed. Every child deserves a good night's sleep—it's vital to their wellbeing. This 'sleep school' program teaches your infant healthy sleep behaviours and the ability to self-settle. If you are reading this book because your child cries for long, unexplained periods of time, you should absolutely consult your doctor to ensure there is no underlying health or emotional issue.

Always, always trust your gut instinct as a parent, and attend to your child if at any point you feel they are in distress. If you are feeling depressed and think you may have postnatal depression, you are not alone. Please call PANDA (Perinatal Anxiety & Depression Australia) on 1300 726 306 (www.panda.org.au) or BeyondBlue on 1300 22 4636 (www.beyondblue.org.au).

Foreword

Mia Freedman

At 3 a.m., no one can hear you scream.

That's precisely how it feels when you're up in the middle of the night with a baby who doesn't sleep. I could hear my baby screaming clearly enough. Several times every night. But my own screams? My screams of exhaustion, despair, frustration and loneliness? They were confined to the inside of my head.

For the first few weeks after my daughter was born, I ran on a heady mix of hormones and adrenaline, with a generous splash of gratitude that my longed-for baby had arrived safely.

Night feeds were almost a novelty. I felt womanly and invincible, filled with love for my little girl and the world. I willingly slept on a crappy mattress on the floor of her room so my beloved husband could sleep undisturbed in our giant bed. I was so grateful to him for helping create this beautiful creature that it was the least I could do. I was a happy martyr. And hey, since I was breastfeeding and he didn't have breasts, what was the point of him getting up at 2 a.m.? Let alone 3, 4 and 5 a.m.

But after more than a month of waking several times every night to feed and soothe my tiny daughter back to sleep, I began to lose my sense of humour.

The adrenaline had long worn off, replaced by an overwhelming fatigue that was crushing the life out of me.

Most mornings I couldn't recall what had transpired the previous night. I was always certain it had been a train wreck but the details were hazy. Did she wake at 1.15 a.m. for a feed, at 2.25 for the dummy, for another feed at 3.10 and then the dummy again at 3.40? Or was it 1.50 a.m. for a feed, 3.20 for the dummy, a feed again at 4.15, and dummy at 4.35 and 5.50? Or was that the night before? Or maybe last week? What's my name again? And who is that person in the mirror? I don't recognise her anymore.

Despair is the evil twin of sleep deprivation. Despair that your baby might never sleep more than a few hours in a row. Despair that you'll never ever feel human again. Despair that no one will ever understand how pitifully exhausted you are. Despair that there's no way out.

It's easier to just stick in the dummy or the bottle or the boob or bring your baby into your bed . . . whatever it takes to get them— and you—back to sleep quickly. After months of broken sleep, a quick fix will always win over the hard yards of a proper solution. You're just too exhausted to find a way out of your exhaustion.

I'd already made this mistake once before, with my son. We had attempted controlled crying half-heartedly a few times but I refused to persevere because I worried it might damage him psychologically. So we waved the white flag and surrendered to the massive disruption of sleeplessness.

In hindsight, this was such a false emotional economy. He didn't sleep properly until he was four and it caused huge stress in our relationship, compromised my ability to go to work and to function properly on some pretty basic levels. Most devastatingly, it leeched chunks of my joy and confidence in being a mother. My husband and I swore we'd do it differently next time.

I should note at this point that both parents do it tough, even if it's only one of you that's bearing the brunt of night waking. Although, after a long night walking the floor with a crying baby, it's funny how hearing your partner say 'I'm tired' when they wake at 7 a.m. can make you want to pick up the nearest heavy object and harm them with it.

Every morning, a shattered parent needs an enormous injection of cheerleading and validation, along the lines of 'You are amazing! You are a hero! You are incredible! I don't know how you do it!' Frequently, even this is not enough to stem the demoralising effects of sleep-deprivation or prevent the resentment from building.

I often felt that nothing short of a ticker-tape parade should be held for me each morning to celebrate my heroism in getting through yet another night. **Yet. Another. Night.**

Invariably, if your baby doesn't sleep, every other baby in your orbit will have begun sleeping through the night from two weeks of age. This will make you feel fantastic. 'People lie' a baby healthcare nurse once assured me when I asked in desperation why I had the only baby in Australia, and possibly the world, who didn't sleep.

Two of my closest friends had babies within a couple of months of me and, despite the fact that one baby did indeed begin sleeping through the night at six weeks, we were each other's solace. Every morning we'd exchange calls or texts detailing what we could remember of the night before.

After particularly bad nights, when one of us would be in the depths of despair, emergency gourmet-food supplies would be left silently at the front door. Meal preparation is one of the first domestic casualties of sleep deprivation and new motherhood. This food was a godsend. The support, even more so.

It was from one of these friends that I first heard about Elizabeth Sloane. She had magical powers to make babies sleep through the night, or so it seemed. My friend had used this sleep whisperer a few years ago with her first baby and Elizabeth had also worked miracles for other mums we knew.

My first conversation with Elizabeth was when my daughter, Coco, was four months old. At that stage, she was waking up as much as eight times a night for feeds and to have her dummy plugged back in. I was beside myself. The feeling of dread began every evening as the sun went down and the inevitability of yet another excruciating night of sleep interruption loomed over me.

It reminded me of labour in a way, when the pain of a contraction can be made worse by the knowledge that there are dozens more lining up behind it. There seemed to be no end to this. No prospect of a solution, of a night where I could sleep more than a couple of hours in a row. And the thought made me panic.

I felt trapped, helpless, hopeless.

Over the phone, Elizabeth was a fount of empathy. Even her voice was soothing. But she was adamant that she wouldn't do a 'sleep program', as she called it, before a baby was six months old. Her belief was that younger babies couldn't really learn to sleep through the night and it was not good for them emotionally. As disappointed as I was, this made me trust Elizabeth even more. The last thing I wanted was to damage my daughter. I just wanted *desperately* to sleep.

Still, I may have lied about Coco's age—cough—a wee bit so Elizabeth would book me in earlier. Which she did, at five and a half months. The day before Elizabeth was due to arrive, she texted me. 'Just checking you still want me to come for the sleep program tomorrow night?' I texted back so fast I nearly broke my thumbs. 'YES! YES! YES!'

The next morning, she called. 'Tonight I'll be there at six so I can meet Coco before we get started. That first night can be pretty intense, so be prepared for that.'

Gulp.

'On the other nights, I'll come at ten and each morning I'll leave at six. Before I go, I'll leave you a report detailing how she went. You can read it when you wake up. I usually crack it in three nights, but I'll pencil in a couple more just in case.'

That evening, after her bath, I dressed Coco in her PJs feeling a mix of apprehension and hope. It was not unlike taking your baby for immunisations: you know it's for their good but your heart is still heavy with guilt for the short-term pain they have to endure.

I liked Elizabeth immediately.

With three small boys of her own and a kind yet no-nonsense attitude, she arrived dressed for the cold winter night ahead.

Straight away, she busied herself in Coco's room as my husband, Jason, and I sat nervously watching. She modified the bedding, removed the mobile from the cot—'Beds are for sleeping not entertainment'—and made sure the room temperature was correct. She was very sweet with Coco and answered my 84 angsty questions. I was tense but she put me at ease as I listened and learned.

All sleep props (things your baby has become reliant upon in order to get to sleep) were to be banished, including dummies, music, bottles, rocking or patting. And boobs. No more milk in the night.

Babies of this age don't need to be fed during the night, I learned. It's habit, not necessity.

The key to success, Elizabeth told us, was that we had to trust her and not crack under the pressure of our baby's cries. Elizabeth believed that, by teaching Coco to put herself to sleep, we were giving her a valuable lifelong gift. This was certainly much more palatable to me than the idea that I was doing it for my own benefit. Lifelong gift? Sold.

And then it was time. I kissed my smiling daughter goodnight with the sense that I was sending her into battle. And after twenty minutes of screaming, the first report from the frontline was not good. 'Your daughter has one of the most extreme dummy addictions I've ever seen,' Elizabeth announced gravely.

Super. Six months old and battling her first addiction. Did that make me her dealer? I had supplied Coco with her first dummy at four weeks and encouraged her descent from casual dummy user to hardcore addict. The instant comfort (hers) and the instant peace (mine) provided by the dummy were sublime.

The mere act of buying dummies would calm me. In these dark, sleepless months, they'd replaced shoes as the object of my retail therapy.

Through the crying, Elizabeth would go in at various intervals and kindly whisper, 'Shhhh, Coco. Time for sleep.' Then she'd re-tuck the sheets firmly and leave without picking Coco up or giving her a bottle. Often she wouldn't actually leave but simply hide in the darkness and observe, making sure Coco didn't get into any serious difficulty.

Jason and I retreated to the lounge with a bottle of wine and turned the TV up loud. Thirty-five minutes after she'd been put to bed, the first hurdle was cleared. Asleep! High five! But while Elizabeth was pleased, she warned us that Coco hadn't really learned anything yet; she was simply exhausted. The night waking would be tougher, she cautioned.

At 10.30 p.m., we went to bed ourselves. We were nervous but relieved that Coco was in the capable hands of a professional. As promised, the night was worse; almost two hours of screaming from 1 a.m. to 3 a.m. I had complete faith in Elizabeth so I was reasonably calm, but still tortured. I didn't cry though, and I didn't interfere.

Lifelong gift. Lifelong gift.

At Elizabeth's suggestion, I stayed in bed, switched on the TV and distracted myself with *E! True Hollywood Story: American Pie*. As I watched Tara Reid's sad journey from starlet to rehab, my husband made sleepy protests about the volume so I hit him on the head with a pillow.

Finally, all was quiet. Next thing, Elizabeth was letting herself out at 6 a.m., followed 45 minutes later by Coco waking up for the day. When I picked her up, I half expected to see betrayal in her eyes, as if to say, 'So where the hell were you last night, bitch?' But her face was as open and delighted to see me as ever. She appeared undamaged. *Lifelong gift*.

Night two was better. I put Coco down myself at 6.30, prop-free, and after some low-level crying, she was asleep in less than ten minutes. Could this be the beginning of a new life for us? One with sleep in it?

Elizabeth arrived at 10 p.m. and we had a cup of tea together. I learned that she loved her work. The lifelong-gift stuff wasn't a platitude; she resolutely believed that every baby deserved to learn how to put themselves to sleep, and that every family deserved the knock-on benefits.

Every week, she told me, she arrived on the doorstep of families in a state of utter emotional and physical chaos, brought on by a baby or child with sleep problems. At the less extreme end, occupied by families like mine, she routinely encountered people driven witless by the destructive cocktail of exhaustion and frustration. Couples bickered. Older children were snapped at. The dog was proverbially kicked.

But within days of the baby leaning to sleep, the family would be transformed. And the babies? What was remarkable, Elizabeth had discovered, was how much happier the babies were. 'People often say to me, "I thought I had a happy baby before, but he's a different baby now that he's sleeping through the night."'

Adults and babies are the same. Everyone is happier after a decent sleep.

And so it was with Coco. The second night was a vast improvement on the first. Forty minutes of crying at 2 a.m. but with nowhere near the intensity of the night before. What was most encouraging was that Coco awoke briefly again at 4 a.m. and put herself back to sleep within a couple of minutes.

Night three she slept through. For the first time in six months, I didn't leave my bed between the hours of 10 p.m. and 6.30 a.m. It was a miracle. Coco was definitely happier during the day. And me? I was doing wild victory laps around my house, positively giddy with the intoxicating feeling of a full night's sleep.

Confident that she'd nailed it, Elizabeth decided her work with Coco was done but left me strict instructions. It was vital that Coco have her proper naps during the day so as not to become overtired—a classic obstruction to sleep. And we had to remember this: now that our baby had endured an undeniably tough few nights, it wasn't fair to her if we undid everything she'd learned with 'just one bottle' or 'just one cuddle' if she woke during the night. Hold firm. Be strong.

And we were. I texted Elizabeth daily for the first week or two with many, many questions and she gave me strength, encouragement and advice. Don't waver. Don't be discouraged if she slips back a little and begins waking occasionally. Have faith that she'll get herself back to sleep eventually. Stick to the rules. Listen and interpret. Comfort and leave.

So changed was our life by Elizabeth's visit, I became utterly evangelical about my genius sleep whisperer. As word spread about my experience, friends of friends began to contact me for her number. They still do. For the first few weeks after Elizabeth came, every morning felt like a miracle. Like Christmas. But slowly, imperceptibly, the unimaginable happened: I began to take my sleep for granted. I went to bed without dread and with the expectation of a full night's sleep.

Two years later, when I had my third child, I texted Elizabeth from the hospital.

'Make a diary note for six months from today, please! I have another one for you!'

The experience of having Elizabeth come and sleep-train Remy was as wonderful as the first time she had come into our lives, and it got me thinking. Not everyone is as fortunate as we were to have Elizabeth. Not everyone can afford it and, even if they could, Elizabeth's ability to help desperate families like mine was limited by geography and time. She only had so many hours in the day, and travelling wasn't an option.

That's where the idea for this book came from.

If you are a sleepless, desperate mother or father looking for some help, support and constructive, detailed advice about helping your baby (or toddler!) sleep, you're in the right place.

Pour yourself a cup of tea (or strong coffee—or wine!) and discover Elizabeth Sloane's Gift Of Sleep.

Sweet dreams,
Mia xxxx

Mia Freedman is the founder and publisher of women's website Mamamia.com.au. Having built her career around creating communities of women in magazines (as Editor of *Cosmopolitan*, and then Editor-in-Chief of *Cosmopolitan*, *Cleo* and *Dolly*) and then a blink-and-you-missed-it stint in commercial TV, Mia wanted to work in a medium that was fast and authentic. So she moved online and began Mamamia.

She is a passionate advocate for positive body image and was the founding chairperson of the National Body Image Advisory Group. Mia also launched parenting site ivillage.com.au which, along with Mamamia, reaches 2 million Australian women each month.

Mia also makes regular appearances on *The Today Show*, *Mornings* and *The Project*. She's written three books, including *The New Black*, *Mamamia: A memoir of mistakes, magazines and motherhood* and *Mia Culpa: Confessions from the watercooler of life*. Mia's husband, Jason, is the CEO of Mamamia (the marriage came before the business) and they have three children and a dog.

Chapter 1

Who is Elizabeth Sloane?

Guardian angel.

Lifesaver.

Sleep whisperer.

Sleep magician.

Baby guru.

Baby whisperer.

Marriage saver.

I'm Elizabeth Sloane, and these are just some of the names I've been called by grateful parents over the past twenty years, as I've had the privilege (and it *is* a privilege) of going into their homes and helping to give their babies, toddlers and even preschoolers the Gift of Sleep.

But the truth is I don't call myself any of those names listed on the previous page. That's because names like 'Baby guru' and 'Magician' make what I do sound mysterious. Difficult. Titles like sleep whisperer make out that I have a special gift—one that *you* don't have—to get your child to sleep. The fact is, that's not true.

What I do isn't magic.
I can teach it to you.

My twenty years of working with babies, toddlers and older children has given me an insight into and knowledge of what they need not just to sleep well (and don't get me wrong—that's a biggie!) but to function. To be happier. To thrive.

In this book I hope to pass on all of that knowledge—all the tips, tricks and strategies I use—to you. Why? So you can become the baby whisperer in your own family. There's no magical fairy dust. No tricks. No spells. Just tips and tools that have worked for me, and the thousands of children I've worked with.

Let me stress: **this book is not about teaching (or forcing) newborns to sleep through the night.** That's not something I condone or personally believe in.

This book is about giving children over the age of six months the gift of sleep. What I mean by that is teaching them how to self-settle.

When a child wakes up and is able to self-settle back to sleep it is a gift. Both for them and for you. Once a child knows how to self-settle, it's a skill that will never leave them.

But I'm getting ahead of myself. First let me share my background with you. I was born in Brisbane. I've always loved babies so it didn't surprise anyone in my family when I decided to study Infant and Maternal Care in the early 80s. That was when I specifically learned settling, lactation and caring for infants and mothers.

Initially I started off teaching new mums how to care for their precious newborns—teaching them how to do everything from bathing their new bub to feeding and settling them. It was a job I loved, and still love.

But an interesting thing started to happen. I began to run into these mums at the shops, say five months down the track, and they'd look shattered. When I asked how things were going, they'd tell me that their beautiful baby was waking up more now than when they were first born. And every chat ended the same way: with these parents asking me to come back and help them get their babies to sleep.

At the same time I was actually raising my own three beautiful sons and the truth was they weren't great sleepers either. So I became a woman with a mission. While continuing to work in this industry, I started researching sleep cycles, sleep behaviour and sleep patterns for babies over six months old. Everything I read told me that the majority of babies over six months of age are perfectly capable of sleeping through the night. So why were so many parents still getting up two, three or five times every night to their crying, grizzling, unsettled children? Good question.

I became passionate about finding the answer; finding a solution to help families struggling with the fatigue and loneliness of having a baby who didn't sleep.

Make no mistake: sleep deprivation slowly unpicks the threads of a family.

Today I have a program that I know works on thriving, healthy children. So if you're at the end of your tether, if you haven't had a decent night's sleep in months (or maybe even years), if the lack of sleep is impacting upon your relationships, your marriage, your job, your emotional wellbeing and let's not forget your children, then this book is for you.

In the following pages, I'm going to teach you how to give your child the gift of sleep. Trust me—it will change your life.

Chapter 2

The case
for and against
controlled crying

If you want to get a group of parents engaged in a lively debate, all you need do is mention two words: controlled crying. It's a verbal hand grenade at any party!

Some parents worship at the Controlled Crying Altar, believing it to be the one thing that restored sleep and sanity to their households. Others view it as a cruel and heartless concept that not only distresses the baby but potentially causes long-term emotional issues.

So who's right?

For starters, **let's define what controlled crying actually is.** Controlled crying (or controlled comforting, as it is sometimes called) is a behavioural technique designed to teach babies to go to sleep, or put themselves back to sleep, independently, without the need for props (think dummies and bottles, and parents having to rock, pat, sing or even feed their babies). A controlled crying program asks parents to leave the crying child alone for set period of time before going to check on and reassure the baby.

The case against controlled crying

The controversy surrounding controlled crying stems from the fact that a number of bestselling 'how to get your baby to sleep' books recommend parents impose such a routine on babies as young as eight weeks old.

This is despite many medical experts recommending that sleep programs not be used on babies younger than six months.

There are also wild variations in the recommendations for how long a child should be left to cry—we're talking anywhere from a few minutes to a full hour.

From a more formal perspective, it would be remiss of me not to mention that in 2004 the Australian Association for Infant Mental Health released a position paper stating its concern for the practice of controlled crying (where 'crying' meant a child in distress rather than the fussing sounds a child makes when settling or adjusting to different circumstances). They also state, 'Although controlled crying can stop children from crying, it may teach children not to seek or expect support when distressed.'

So, does that mean that 'controlled crying' is wrong and shouldn't be advocated?

In my opinion, the important thing is that you do what you feel is right for your family.

The case for controlled crying

In 2010, the Murdoch Childrens Research Institute released the results of a world-first study, which found that behavioural techniques like controlled crying are safe for babies over six months of age.

The study also showed that techniques such as controlled crying, which help babies learn to put themselves to sleep by letting them cry for set periods of time, and positive bedtime routines **had no adverse effects on the emotional and behavioural development of children or their relationship with parents.**

Left untreated, sleep problems can affect up to 45 per cent of babies aged six to twelve months, and can double the mother's risk of postnatal depression.

Without intervention, sleep problems are also more likely to persist into childhood, potentially leading to behavioural and cognitive problems including aggression, anxiety, and attention and learning difficulties.

These findings form part of a longitudinal study by the Murdoch Childrens Research Institute into infant sleep that has shown 'intervention during infancy significantly reduces sleep problems in children and depression among mothers during the first two years of the child's life.' (You can read the full statement on these results in the box below).

CONTROLLED CRYING TECHNIQUE SAFE FOR BABIES

Using behavioural techniques including controlled crying to help infants sleep does not lead to later emotional and behavioural problems, according to new research by the Murdoch Childrens Research Institute.

The world-first study followed up 225 six-year-old children who had received behavioural sleep intervention as babies to assess their health, including emotional wellbeing, behaviour and child–parent relationship.

Lead researcher Anna Price said the study would help reassure parents and health professionals about the safety of sleep interventions in infants aged six months and older, especially as a strategy to prevent and treat postnatal depression. 'Sleep problems can affect up to 45 per cent of babies aged six to twelve months and can double the risk of postnatal depression,' she said.

'Without intervention, sleep problems are also more likely to persist into childhood, potentially leading to behavioural and cognitive problems including aggression, anxiety, and attention and learning difficulties.

'Given that behavioural sleep techniques are cost effective in reducing sleep problems and maternal depression, health professionals can feel comfortable offering these interventions to families presenting with infant sleep problems. Parents can also feel reassured they are not harming their babies by using sleep interventions.'

The findings form part of a longitudinal study by Murdoch Childrens into infant sleep, which has shown intervention during infancy significantly reduces sleep problems in children and depression among mothers during the first two years of the child's life.

(Reproduced with kind permission of the Murdoch Childrens Research Institute)

So what does all this mean? It means that, in the right circumstances and conducted in a loving manner, controlled crying programs can help a child. A lack of sleep, caused by frequent waking in the night and a dependence on Mum or Dad to get back to sleep can affect an infant's development (their gross motor skills), appetite, general wellbeing and happiness, and their ability to socialise. Sleep deprivation can also cause overstimulation and separation anxiety in babies and small children. Every child deserves to be taught how to fall asleep alone and how to drift back to sleep when they wake in the night.

Wherever you stand on the issue, the fact is when faced with a screaming baby (and their own sheer exhaustion), most parents have found themselves at least contemplating leaving the baby to 'cry it out' for a while. Who can blame them? I don't need to tell you that sleep deprivation is a hideous thing. When we feel tired, stressed and overwhelmed, most of us will try anything if it means getting our baby to sleep.

So where does my Gift of Sleep program fit in? And does it use controlled crying techniques? I'm glad you asked.

Chapter 3

What is the Gift of Sleep program and is it right for my baby?

Thinking about your life before kids, would you have called yourself a good sleeper? Did you find it fairly easy to get off to sleep at
night? When you woke during the night were you able to pretty
easily drift back to sleep again?

Being able to self-settle, or to go to sleep without any props or
aids, is not a skill that we're born with. Self-settling is something
we need to learn how to do.

And that is what my Gift of Sleep program is all about.

Giving your child the gift of sleep is
actually all about giving them the gift
of being able to self-settle. And it *is*
a gift—for them and for you.

It's about putting your baby in their cot while they are tired but
still awake, knowing that they will be able to drift off to sleep
without the aid of a parent patting them or rocking them or
singing to them. Without them needing to be breastfed or given
a bottle. Without sitting in a rocking swing or wheeled around

in a pram. Without having a dummy that needs to be replugged six times a night by Mum or Dad!

When babies are able to get themselves off to sleep independently, the benefits are far-reaching. It means that wherever they are—a sleepover at Gran's house or on holiday in a travel cot—they can still drift off to sleep without you needing to lug sound machines or musical mobiles or 50,000 spare dummies along with you.

When I explain all of this to parents, they often ask me why I insist on waiting until a baby is six months old to start my program. Can't we teach a twelve-week-old these skills and restore sleep to the household a bit sooner?

It's a good question.

There are a few reasons why I insist on six months, or at the very least that the baby weighs 8 kilograms.

1 Research tells us that a normal, healthy baby is perfectly able to sleep for twelve hours straight at night once they are six months old. At that age, children do not need a night-time feed.

2 By six months, a baby's sleep patterns have changed and they are going into the heavier, non-REM (rapid eye movement) sleep first. (Younger babies tend to go into the lighter, REM sleep initially, which is why they find it harder to go to sleep and then tend to be 'light sleepers'.)

3 By six months, a baby will have started eating solids. Some babies don't sleep through the night until they have started solids, so it's always a good idea to tick this milestone off first.

4 By six months of age, babies have had all their early vaccinations. Again, by waiting until six months of age, we can rule that out as a reason for them waking during the night.

Does the Gift of Sleep program use controlled crying?

Yes and no. Yes, if you mean allowing babies to grizzle or cry for set periods of time while they learn to self-soothe. You need to be prepared for the fact that your baby will cry. After all, they have become dependent on a sleep prop that we are taking away to teach them how to sleep without it! So your baby will give a cry of 'protest' during the program, but think of it as your baby saying, 'What's going on? I want my dummy/music/patting!' rather than a cry that indicates they are in any type of physical or emotional distress.

I can't stress enough that I do not advocate leaving babies or children to cry for long periods of time. This program is not about shutting the nursery door, walking away and leaving a child to cry itself to sleep. If during the program you feel at any time that something is wrong with your child (other than them doing a 'protest' type of cry) then you should always go to them.

My three-day program is very much about gently and lovingly teaching your baby how to get themself off to sleep independently while still offering them plenty of reassurance that they have not been abandoned.

Let me repeat: my program is not about making your baby sleep through the night—although that is often the result. Instead, my goal is to teach your child to self-settle. I want your baby to know how to go to sleep and I want to ensure they are able to get themselves back to sleep without you if they wake during the night.

Self-settling is the key.

How do I know if this program is right for my child and me?

I'm the first to say that this program isn't for everyone. After all, you need to do what is right for you, your family and your child.

Perhaps getting up during the night for your baby doesn't bother you. If that's the case, then do what works. Keep doing it until you feel it isn't working anymore.

Or perhaps the thought of a three-day program where you have to leave your child to cry for five to ten minutes is just too distressing to even bear thinking about. Again, that's totally OK. There is no judgement from me, as I truly believe that each family needs to do what works for them. We're all different, after all.

However, if you answer yes to one or more of the following questions, you may want to consider coming with me on the Gift of Sleep journey.

- Does your child need you to help them go to sleep? Examples include sleeping in the same bed as you, cuddling, rocking, patting, singing, driving them around the block, or some other method that involves your presence. Most importantly, do you want to change that?
- In order to get to sleep, does your child require a dummy and do you need to replug that dummy during the night?
- Does your child wake up during the night and require you in some form—patting, rocking, cuddles, singing, replugging a dummy—to help them get back to sleep?
- Is sleep deprivation making you feel overwhelmed and affecting your ability to function during the day?
- Is sleep deprivation affecting your partner and your relationship?
- Is sleep deprivation affecting your other children?
- Do you think you may have postnatal depression?

If you answered yes to any of these questions and you feel the desire to change the situation, then the Gift of Sleep program may be for you.

Chapter 4

The nine
Golden Rules

Now, I don't want you to rush into doing a sleep program before you've read through—and agreed to—my Golden Rules. The nine Golden Rules you need to know before committing to my Gift of Sleep program are as follows.

1 **Your baby must be well.** Don't start a sleep program when your child has a cold or any type of illness, as they will understandably be more grizzly and need extra comfort. It's also preferable that you are 100 per cent well too. Before you start a sleep program, I'd advise you to get your paediatrician to confirm that your child is in good health.

2 **You and your partner must *both* be committed to the Gift of Sleep program.** You should both be supportive of the journey you are taking with your baby in order to give them back the gift of sleep. If one of you is unsure about the program, it won't work. You need to be in it together, supporting one another on this journey. If you're a single parent or your partner is away, consider asking a close friend or relative to stay a couple of nights for moral support and to help you stick to the program.

3 **There will be some crying on this program for it to work.** You need to be prepared for this before you begin. After all, your little one has become dependent on a prop to get to sleep,

which isn't fair to them or to you. Yes, you'll have moments of feeling guilty and distressed as you hear your child cry. Just remember that the crying will be short-lived, and the gift of sleep you are giving your child will last them a lifetime.

4 **Talk to your neighbours!** If you are stressed at the thought that your grizzling child may somehow annoy your neighbours, particularly on the first night of the program, give them advance notice. Let them know that you're doing a sleep program and for a night or two there might be a bit of crying, but your baby is absolutely not being neglected.

5 **Choose the right time to do the three-night program.** For many families, it's ideal to start the program on a Friday night so that you have two days over the weekend when your partner (or a friend or relative) is home and able to help. You're also both able to support each other through the ups and downs, as you may be overtired from getting up a lot on the first night. Experience tells me that if one or both parents have to work the day after the first night of the program or be somewhere early, someone will probably cave in. Remove that pressure by choosing a time when you are free of work and outside commitments.

6 **Lie low over the three days of the program.** You and your baby will both be tired as you do sleep school. Don't plan lots of activities over these three days. Your baby will be particularly tired as they get used to this new way of sleeping. It's much better to have a few quieter days at home while you complete the Gift of Sleep program.

7 **Give yourself a 30-day buffer zone at home.** Don't plan to do the Gift of Sleep program when you are away from home or are about to go travelling or move house or environment in the next three weeks. Don't decide to fly to Bali one week after completing the three-day program. You run the risk of undoing all your hard work. It's very important to stay in a stable environment initially to lock it in. Your baby will be sleeping, but they need time to get it right every night. Consistency is key.

8 **Make notes.** (Use the free worksheets at the back of this book.) Be prepared to make quick notes during the three-day program. This is so you can experience and really observe first hand the differences in and the duration of your baby's cry. By taking notes, you'll have something to refer to later and will easily be able to see the progress being made.

9 **If you have a partner, support them—and vice versa.** Try not to blame or second-guess each other during the program. Put past mistakes or cave-ins behind you. Focus on the positive, stick together and remember that you'll look back on this in two nights and say, 'Why did we wait so long?' If you don't have a partner, believe in yourself. You're strong. You're a parent! You can do this.

10 **On the first day of the program, make sure you've fed your baby well.** Make sure that they've had a good evening meal and have been bottle- or breastfed. You may be surprised to know that 95 per cent of bubs over six months do not wake from hunger during the night, but you'll be reassured knowing

your little one ate well that day before going into the first night of the program.

11 **On the first day of the program, make sure your baby is up from their afternoon nap (if they have one!) no later than 4 p.m.**

12 **Before you begin, decide what time in the morning is OK for your baby to wake up and stay awake. (This is the time after which you won't try to get them back to sleep.)** How do you define 'morning'? Is it 6 a.m.? 5.30 a.m.? I think 6 a.m. onwards is totally acceptable. Having said that, I would not pick battles with a baby who woke at 5.30 a.m. during the program. Your baby's little body is adjusting to a new volume of sleep.

13 **Don't embark on any other huge changes in the first few weeks of the program.** Don't decide to toilet-train your toddler or move them to a big bed. Don't have baby injections planned or be attempting to wean your baby off any other habits. Let your baby purely focus on learning these new self-settling habits. Be patient! While your little one is doing this, they will need extra love and support.

14 **And finally, stick to the three Cs: calm, committed, and consistent.**

Chapter 5

The Gift of Sleep program

Preparing the nursery

The first step, before we put your little one to bed for sleep school, is to make sure the nursery is set up the right way.

Temperature

This is probably one of the biggest areas of concern for parents, who worry whether their baby is too hot or too cold. The nursery should be between 19 and 22 degrees Celsius. That being said, don't get caught up in obsessing about the temperature. (And don't rely on those cheap little temperature gauges as they are not always accurate and can give you a false sense of security.) The rule of thumb I use is if *you* feel the temperature has dropped then there's a good chance your baby feels it also. Remember that from six months old babies—like us—self-regulate their body heat. So your baby can wear the same amount of clothing that you wear. If the night suddenly feels humid and muggy, take a layer off your baby's bed. If you feel the temperature drop at night and want to put on a cardigan, chances are your baby feels it too, so add another cotton blanket to their bed. I always like to tuck blankets in under the cot mattress so they don't have a chance to travel during the night.

The colder months

I'm not a big fan of bar heaters but if you do choose to use a low electric bar heater it's imperative that you leave the door ajar. That way if there is a malfunction during the night, when the rest of the family is asleep, the heat will have somewhere to escape.

A better option is a cellular blanket on top of your baby. Safety is the priority, so a lovely stretchy cotton blanket (with breathable holes throughout) is what you want.

The warmer months

I favour oscillating fans in nurseries. The fan blade should be facing towards the wall with a 60-centimetre gap so air can still circulate. No baby should have a fan forcefully moving air around their body. All we want to do on very warm nights is keep the air flowing, and a fan facing the wall will do that well and safely. Fans are also considerably cheaper than air-conditioners, which inevitably move to extreme temperatures and are harder to regulate.

The humming noise of an air-conditioner is also very soothing and can inadvertently become a prop for your baby to sleep. This is fine if you're at home with it on, but not so fine if you're visiting the grandparents or on holiday!

Sleeping bags

There are a number of baby sleeping bags, like Plum sleepbags or Grobag, on the market, and my advice is to go for cotton. So what weight should you get in your sleeping bag? In summer, 0.5 to 1.0 tog is perfect. In winter months, up to 4 tog is appropriate.

If your baby is a wriggler, try to make sure the bag has lots of legroom and don't be afraid to go up a size. You want at least 10 centimetres of free legroom from where your baby's feet sit to the bottom of the bag.

Lighting

Bright lights startle babies during the night so what you want is a small night light or a dim bedside lamp that you can put on when you want to check on your baby. Even an outside hall light can work. Bright lights being flicked on during the night are inevitably associated with sleep problems, and our aim is to be able to move in and out of the nursery without baby noticing.

Make sure the lights in your baby's room are not shining in their eyes. If you need to reposition the cot so that it's not directly under a light, do that. It could also be worth getting a dimmer switch put on your main bedroom light. It's inexpensive and allows you to control the level of light while you tiptoe into and out of the nursery during the night.

The cot

The cot base should be dropped and the mattress should be flat (so not elevated in any form). This reduces any risk of the baby falling out of the cot.

In keeping with SIDS (sudden infant death syndrome, or cot death) guidelines, remove any cot bumpers and pillows. We want to encourage ventilation and reduce the risk of SIDS through baby suffocating against a bumper or pillow.

Pillows should not be used until your child is in a big-girl or big-boy bed.

Next, remove the mattress protector; I truly believe the plastic backing on them makes babies sweat. They can definitely be a reason why a baby is overheating, especially when babies sleep on their backs, where they retain a lot of heat. Let's get your child sleeping well first and you can always reintroduce a mattress protector later on down the track. If you're worried about the mattress being ruined, you can go for a cotton mattress protector with no plastic backing.

Cot positioning is important. Try to move the cot to a corner of the room that isn't close to the door or in the path of a lot of light. Babies are very sensitive to noise in the first week of a sleep program, when their little bodies are adjusting to a new volume of sleep. You also want the cot in a spot where you can visually check on your baby without having to walk into the room.

Cot sheets

Your baby's sheets need to be 100 per cent cotton. This is very important and adheres to SIDS guidelines. You'll find that cotton sheets are cooler because they breathe well, and they are easy to wash. They're also usually quicker to dry than many synthetic blends. It's a good idea to have a spare set of cot sheets and a fresh sleeping bag on hand in the nursery in case there are any accidents (vomiting or a leaked nappy) during the nights of the program.

Mobiles and toys

Gone! Cots are for sleeping, not entertaining! Your baby's imagination and the general environment of the nursery will provide more than enough joy and stimulation for them as their little minds wander and relax. Anything more than that can distract and overstimulate them and be a barrier to sleep.

Let your baby have a 'sleep friend'

OK, now that I've told you to get rid of the toys in the cot, I want you to **let your baby have one sleep friend—a special toy that gives them comfort.** Having a sleep friend is very important in the long-term for babies from six months of age onwards. It's not hugely important to the success of my Gift of Sleep program, but **it is essential for your child's wellbeing, and for them to remain outstanding sleepers and on track.**

For instance, if your baby gets sick a sleep friend in the cot will provide them with comfort. Similarly when going through the shock of separation when starting daycare or the arrival of a new baby, extended family, or a new nanny or babysitter, a sleep friend can provide valuable familiarity in a little person's life. Their sleep friend will remind them of home.

Let me say that I do prefer the sleep friend remain in bed or be kept in the kindy or daycare bag and brought out only for sleep. This reduces the chance of the sleep friend getting lost or accumulating too many germs from day-to-day life. If you can afford it, you may want to stock up on a couple in case one gets lost.

Whatever toy you choose as your baby's sleep friend, just make sure it's safe—so no eyes or buttons or ribbons could fall off—and that it is replaceable.

The three Cs

There are three words that guide everything I do with children: calm, committed and consistent.

Calm

If you can stay calm—even when your child has been awake all night, or has just used your new lipstick as a crayon to draw on the walls—you will make better decisions and your emotions won't escalate the situation. Keeping calm with babies is key since children respond to the emotions you give out. Staying calm helps keep babies calm.

Committed

It's important that you stick to the Gift of Sleep program once you start. If you are serious about giving your baby the gift of sleep, then you need to commit to my program 100 per cent.

There really is no point if you give up after the first few hours. It's not fair to your baby. Stay committed and the program will pay off for you and your household.

Consistent

Then there's the need for parents to be consistent. Start as you mean to continue. We all know (usually from trial and error) how confusing it is for children of all ages if we are constantly changing the goal posts on them, be it with bedtime routines or teenage curfews. Kids and babies love predictability. When you are learning all day long, as babies and toddlers in particular are, there is something soothing about having a routine. Routine makes kids feel secure. Each day can be full of surprises for babies and small children, but routines and consistency help them to relax. Imagine them thinking as their bedtime routine starts, 'Oh, I know what's happening now. Mummy is going to read me two stories and then tuck me into bed with my bear. I can relax.'

Beginning the Gift of Sleep program

The importance of a bedtime routine

I can't say it enough. Sleep—or, more precisely, the lack of sleep—is the number one difficulty faced by all the thousands of parents I have spoken with over the years. So if you're reading this and you feel overwhelmed, stressed out and at the end of your rope, you're not alone. *You are not alone.* I promise you that. We can change things for the better, but I want to stress how important it is that, if you embark on this journey of restoring sleep to your household, you need to keep going. Stay consistent. Don't put in the work over the three nights of the program then go back to old habits or send mixed messages to your baby. Start as you mean to continue. Stick to my advice.

Always remember that babies thrive on routine, routine, routine.

If you get off track, regroup the next night. *Do not* let old habits slip back. Your baby needs you to stay consistent and calm. Leave the rest to your baby and watch them shine. Babies do not come with a manual on how to sleep through the night; it is a skill they learn with planning, patience and love.

Now, before you start the bedtime routine below, I want you to take all the props out of your baby's nursery. The dummies. The music. Anything that your child has been using to get to sleep. Because at 3 a.m., I don't want you to cave in, in a moment of weakness.

The routine

My Gift of Sleep program begins with the baby's first night-time sleep. I've already talked about the importance of routines and consistency. Well, first up, I want you to follow the same routine every night when you put your baby down to sleep.

We're going to begin with a bedtime story. I favour a small lamp and chair in the nursery as well as a little shelf of storybooks. I think it's important during the Gift of Sleep program that the same person puts the baby down each night. What you want is to establish a routine. Babies *love* routines. Routines are your key to success. The sleep friend can be removed from the cot and placed with the baby on your lap while you read the bedtime story.

The key during story time is to keep the environment calm and quiet. Don't read the story in front of the TV. Leave your phone somewhere else. Go into the quiet nursery and keep things calm as this will lead to a calmer and happier transfer when baby leaves your arms to go in the cot.

The bedtime routine for a baby who is aged six to eleven months might look something like this:

5.30 p.m.	Bath time
5.45 p.m.	Baby massage, fresh nappy and get dressed for bed
6.00 p.m.	Bottle or breastfeed
6.10 p.m.	Dress in sleeping bag
6.15 p.m.	Bedtime story in the bedroom, low lighting, sleep friend
6.25 p.m.	Place the baby in bed, saying, 'Time for bed now, Georgie.'
6.30 p.m.	Switch off the lamp and say goodnight

For twelve- to eighteen-month-olds, push the routine start time forward half an hour to 6 p.m.

Keep in mind that this first settle (putting your baby to bed in a new way and without props) is often the most challenging. If you can get this one under your belt, you'll realise your baby has gone down without aids or manual settling.

OK, here we go . . .

The Gift of Sleep

program for babies aged

six to eleven months

The first night

Step 1

Place your baby in their sleeping bag. Make sure their nappy is dry and clean before placing them into the cot. There is no need to change your baby's nappy during the night unless they have done a poo, and this usually stops once night feeding stops.

Step 2

As per SIDS (sudden infant death syndrome, or cot death) guidelines, place your baby on their back to sleep.

Step 3

Place the sleep friend (see page 53) somewhere near your baby, preferably near their cheek or face but not too close. It can take a few weeks for a baby at only six months old to form a friendship with their special sleeping toy, but it *will* happen and it will be an ongoing source of comfort for your baby.

Step 4

Tuck your baby in! Yep, I want you to tuck the bag in at the bottom of the cot so that your baby is nice and secure. Place a cotton sheet across baby's chest like a large band and tuck it firmly under the base of the cot sides. Why? Well, what you want is for your baby to feel the pressure when they cry and arch up. I find ths promotes self-settling quicker and is a great trigger for sleep.

Keep in mind though that both of these methods of tucking your baby in are temporary measures just to be used during the nights of the sleep program. I have found most babies self-settle quicker when their position is secure. This is also very helpful for programs where parents are struggling to get rid of wraps.

Step 5

By now your baby will be in what I call the 'star position' with their arms free above the tucked-in sheet, and their legs tucked under the sheet. Your baby might also be crying (and fair enough too!) if they are not used to this new sleeping position, and have not been given their old props (like a dummy or a breastfeed).

OK. Breathe. Stay calm. Leave the room. We're now going to do what I call the five-minute wait, knock and re-settle.

Wait five minutes outside baby's room—but no more **than five minutes!** Babies are still so little at six months old and you want to send the message that you are on the journey with them.

After five minutes, peek through the nursery door and visually check on your baby. Is baby OK? This is more for your peace of mind than anything else, so you can be reassured that this new strategy is not harming your baby at all.

Next, knock loudly—very loudly—on the nursery door for 30 seconds. Why? This sound lowers a baby's breathing and calms them down so that hopefully they will move to a lower volume of crying. (If your baby does not respond or lower their cry when you knock, you can try a loud 'Shhhhh!' five times for about 30 seconds and then stop.) Your tone should be firm but loving. Definitely not angry! Remember this is your first re-settle and it is going to be challenging. I want you to stay calm and confident. Don't think of this as controlled crying—it is 'comfort settling' or even 'progressive waiting'. You are teaching your baby to sleep independently, to self-settle, and that is a gift.

Now what you need to do is listen and start paying attention to your baby's different cries. Use the worksheets at the end of this book. If by the end of these five minutes of knocking or shushing, your baby is doing a stop-start cry, it means they are calming down. Lie low and wait silently for another five minutes. This is so you don't miss the window of opportunity if your baby is self-settling. However, if your baby's cry has escalated in volume and pitch then go into the nursery to re-settle them.

The re-settle

When you re-settle, it's important that you don't talk or even make eye contact with your baby. Absolutely don't pick your baby up or offer any of the usual props like dummies or patting.

Simply go in, re-tuck your baby's sheet and again say in a firm but loving tone, 'Shhhh' five times and then leave the room. Wait another five minutes outside the nursery. If your baby's crying continues at the same level, keep doing the loud knock or shushing for 30 seconds to one minute.

Now's a good time to remind yourself of the findings from the Murdoch Childrens Research Institute: sleep programs for babies over the age of six months do not cause the baby any damage, and 'Without intervention, sleep problems are also more likely to persist into childhood, potentially leading to behavioural and cognitive problems including aggression, anxiety and attention and learning difficulties.'

I know that your baby can do this.
Have faith in your baby, and have faith
in your own ability.

Now back to another five-minute wait. If during this second set of crying your baby's cry lowers to a stop-start grizzle then lie low and extend your quiet wait to **seven minutes**. Do this in case there is a window of opportunity that your baby will self-settle and drift off to sleep.

Don't be disappointed if your baby doesn't go to sleep without some protest—it's completely normal, and understandable from the baby's point of view. Things have changed and they want to say, 'Hang on! What's going on here?' But remember, we've just started this journey! It takes an average of 30 minutes for most babies to settle on this program. In some stronger bubs this first re-settle can take up to one hour.

Step 6

Repeat the five-minute wait, knock and re-settle as needed. So again after five minutes knock slowly and loudly, or shush, from the nursery door for 30 seconds to one minute. Wait another five minutes and keep assessing your baby's cry. Are they calming down? If not, and the cry is escalating, go in to the nursery and do a re-settle. Then go back and wait outside the nursery door.

Continue this until your baby is asleep. Keep filling in your worksheets so that you can look back and see that you are making progress.

Don't be concerned if your baby hasn't fallen asleep in the star position. Let's face it, once babies can roll over they are able to find their own comfortable sleeping position.

You may find that your baby eventually falls asleep out of exhaustion, but be assured that baby will reward you with a quicker settle next week. Why? Because you have implemented a new routine to which baby will quickly adapt.

This first night is by far the most challenging. Like most parents, you are sure to feel anxious and distressed at hearing your baby cry. You'll probably feel a mixture of guilt, concern and distress. Just remember that your baby is safe from harm and is simply protesting about the change in sleeping arrangements. Whatever you do, don't put baby through five minutes of crying then send them mixed signals that undermine the program. It will take much longer, and unnecessarily upset your baby, if you only do the program half-heartedly.

Your baby doesn't just deserve to get a good night's sleep—they need it.

Now, prepare yourself for the exact same routine for the rest of the night. Wait for five minutes, then knock slowly and loudly on the nursery door, or shush, for 30 seconds to one minute and then go into the room to re-settle. You must expect, in order for baby to get the best learning done, that this will be a busy night. My preference would be that one of you does this first night while the other person gets some rest. Then the rested person can take over in the morning while the other rests.

If your baby hasn't gone to sleep after 30 to 45 minutes and you are feeling distressed and overwhelmed, go into the nursery, pick baby up and take them outside into, say, the lounge (just make sure the lighting is dim) and give them a loving cuddle for a few minutes. You'll feel reassured because baby will immediately stop crying and you'll see that your precious bundle is totally fine and is simply protesting the change in routine! Now . . . *do not* revert to old habits! Don't offer dummies or a breastfeed or whatever sleep prop your child is addicted to. Just give baby a cuddle and, after a few minutes, place them back in the cot and keep going with the program.

The next day

Both you and your baby will be feeling tired today, and maybe a little fragile. That's OK. You've had a big night of learning, and baby has started to adjust to a new, healthy sleep routine. So lie low today. Don't plan to do lots of activities that will make baby even more tired or overstimulated. Have a quiet day at home and watch your baby for tired cues and get them into bed for their nap ahead of time.

What about day sleeps?

The moment you see your baby showing signs of tiredness, get them in for their nap. You definitely don't want baby to become overtired. In terms of routine, day sleeps are the same. You place your bub in their sleeping bag in the star position then leave the room, wait for five minutes and then knock loudly or shush from the nursery door for 30 seconds to one minute. Baby will cry when your knock or shushing stops but their cry will drop back each time until they self-settle.

The truth is that day sleeps can be hit-and-miss for the first few weeks after you start the sleep program. I tend to treat daytime sleeps as negotiable, but **not the nights.** And I firmly believe you will never lock daytime sleeps in until the night sleep is locked in.

When a baby wakes up fully rested, you have a better chance of getting them to sleep during the day. An overtired baby is fractious and finds it even harder to get to sleep, no matter how tired they may be.

So with that in mind, let's stick to one rule with the daytime sleeps. As long as baby is going down independently in the star position then you are on track. If baby wakes after less than an hour you can try a re-settle from the door. If, after two attempts at the five-minute wait, knock and re-settle, baby is still crying, get them up. You don't want baby crying a lot in the day, given that at night you are not in a position to pick them up.

The second night

The second night of the program should be similar to the first but I would expect less crying and a quicker response from baby. Having said that, please don't be despondent if that is not the case. Don't second-guess the program. Your baby can do this, and so can you. Remember that I have worked with thousands of babies over the years and I can say that—assuming your baby is healthy—your baby is not the first one who cannot sleep through the night.

Don't make the mistake of suddenly blaming teething or hunger for your baby's wakefulness. Remember the issue is nearly always behavioural and usually stems from a sleep association like a dependence on patting or a dummy or being fed to sleep.

This second night is also about slightly extending the time frame of listening to your baby's cry. Trust me, on the second night the cry is not as distressing. So on the second night, try a progressive wait before you knock. Aim for a ten-minute wait. If your baby doesn't move to self-settle or start a stop-start grizzle, then do the knock for 30 seconds to one minute. If the crying escalates in pitch and volume, go into the nursery to re-settle your baby. Keep in mind that you ultimately want to phase out the knocking or shushing to help promote self-settling.

The third night

In my experience, 70 per cent of babies will be well and truly going down to bed more calmly by the third night, and most are sleeping through the night or, at the very least, self-settling when they do wake up. You are on the home stretch! Stay confident and focused.

Remember that this program is *not* about teaching your baby to sleep through the night without waking at all (though that does usually happen). It's about baby knowing how to self-settle so that if they do wake up during the night, they are able to get themselves back to sleep.

If your baby is still waking up distressed, repeat the instructions from the second night. After all, every baby and family is different. Your baby will get there in their own time.

My program runs for three nights, but some babies will take five nights. But trust me, babies respond beautifully as long as you, the parent, stay calm, committed and consistent. If you don't remain consistent, you will confuse your baby and they may revert to old behaviours.

As I've said before, it is always distressing to hear your little one cry, but keep reminding yourself that your baby is safe and well and that their cry is simply one of protest. In my opinion, it's simply not fair to make a child dependent on you or a prop in order to sleep. What happens if they to spend a night away from you? Your child needs to be able to sleep without totally relying on your presence.

So stay strong. Remind yourself that what you're doing is giving your child a lifelong gift of being a great sleeper.

The Gift of Sleep program

for babies aged twelve to

eighteen months

This program is specifically for babies who are standing and very mobile in the cot. These bubs are moving in and around the cot. The good news is that, in my experience, this age group is the quickest to learn my Gift of Sleep program. Also, following SIDS safe sleeping guidelines, you can now safely put your baby to sleep on their tummy. This is particularly good news, as babies tend to settle much faster when placed on their tummies to sleep.

The first night

Step 1

Follow the bedtime routine for babies aged six to eleven months on page 59, pushing the start time back to 6 p.m.

Step 2

Place your baby in their sleeping bag. Make sure their nappy is dry and clean before placing the baby into the cot. There is no need to change their nappy during the night unless they have done a poo, and this usually stops once night feeding stops.

Step 3

Place your baby in what I call the 'reverse star position' at the bottom end of the cot. This means they are to be on their tummy. Let me reassure you that once babies are twelve months old, it is safe to put them to sleep on their tummies thanks to their neck and head strength and the fact that they independently move around the cot. (If you have any concerns about your child's neck and head strength or are at all concerned about putting them to bed on their tummy, you should consult your child health nurse or paediatrician before starting this program).

Now, tuck your baby in if you can. Tuck the excess material at the end of the sleeping bag under the end of the cot mattress. If your baby isn't too strong, use a sheet to try to keep them from standing up. Place a cotton sheet like a large band across baby's lower back and tuck it firmly under the base of the cot sides. What you want is for baby to feel the pressure when they cry and arch up. I find this promotes self-settling quicker.

Remember, these methods of tucking your child in are both temporary measures. I usually stop tucking the sleeping bag in and remove the sheet after the first week, once the program is locked in. It's a little trick I'm happy to share with you, but just remember it's a temporary strategy. Your baby is mobile and will be roaming around the cot and settling in all sorts of positions you never imagined. But I have found that most babies learn to self-settle quicker on their tummies and when their position is secure.

If your baby continues to stand at the end of the cot, the experience can go on for an unacceptable amount of time. If you can keep baby immobilised and flat, this will ease the transition to self-settling. If baby is simply too strong and frees themself from the sheet (which most babies can do after twelve months) then don't be too concerned.

Step 4

Place the sleep friend (see page 53) somewhere near baby.

Step 5

By now your baby is probably crying (and fair enough too!) as they are not used to this new sleeping position or to being without their old props (like a dummy or a breastfeed).

OK. Breathe. Stay calm. Leave the room. We're now going to do the five-minute wait, knock and re-settle.

Wait five minutes outside baby's room, **but no more than five minutes!** Your baby is still so little and you want to send the message that you are on the journey with them.

After five minutes, I want you to peek through the nursery door and visually check on your baby. **Their head should be turned to the side or resting on their hands.** Next, knock loudly—very loudly—on the door for 30 seconds. Why? This sound will lower baby's breathing and calms them down so that hopefully they will move to a lower volume of cry. If, by chance, your baby does not respond or lower their cry when you knock, you can try loudly sayng, 'Shhhh' five times for about 30 seconds and then stop. Your tone should be firm but loving. Definitely not angry! Remember this is your first re-settle and it is going to be challenging. I want you to stay calm and confident. Don't think of this as controlled crying—it is 'comfort settling' or even 'progressive waiting'. You are teaching your baby to sleep independently, to self-settle, and that is a gift.

Now what you need to do is listen and start paying attention to your baby's different cries. Use the worksheets at the end of this book. If by the end of five minutes of knocking or shushing, baby is doing a stop-start cry that means they are calming down, so lie low and wait silently for another five minutes. This is so you don't miss the window of opportunity if your baby is self-settling.

However, if your baby's cry has escalated in volume and pitch, or if they are standing in the cot, then go into the nursery to re-settle them.

The re-settle

Go into the nursery but make no eye contact with your baby and provide no stimulation (so no talking). Gently remove your crying bub from their standing or sitting position, lie them down and tuck the base of their sleeping bag back into the mattress to encourage them to stay in the reverse star position on their tummies. And remember, don't crack or offer any props. No dummies, patting or bottles!

Then say to your baby in a firm but loving tone, 'Shhhh!' five times and leave the room.

Now I want you to wait five minutes and then say 'Shhhh!' five times again, but this time stand by the nursery door. Again, keep your tone firm but loving.

Now's a good time to remind yourself of the findings of the Murdoch Childrens Research Institute study. Sleep programs for babies over the age of six months do not cause the baby any damage. And:

'Without intervention, sleep problems are also more likely to persist into childhood, potentially leading to behavioural and cognitive problems including aggression, anxiety and attention and learning difficulties.'

I know that your baby can do this. So can you! Have faith.

Don't be disappointed if your baby doesn't go to sleep. You've just started this journey! And listen, it takes an average of 30 minutes for most babies to settle. In some stronger bubs this first re-settle can take up to one hour.

Step 6

Repeat the five-minute wait, knock and re-settle as needed. So again after five minutes knock slowly and loudly on the nursery door, or shush, for 30 seconds to one minute. If your baby's crying escalates, go in and do a re-settle. Then go back outside and wait another five minutes, and either do the knock or shush from the door. Continue this way until baby is asleep. You may find that your baby eventually falls asleep out of exhaustion, but be assured that they will reward you with a quicker settle tomorrow.

If your baby just keeps busting out of their reverse star position and is continually standing up in the cot like a jack-in-the-box you can consider very, very gently placing your hands on their back and/or bottom when you do the re-settle just to help soothe them into this new sleeping position while they relax and get used to being on their tummy.

This first night is by far the most challenging. Like most parents, you are sure to feel anxious and distressed at hearing your baby cry. You'll probably feel a mixture of guilt, concern and distress. Just remember that your baby is safe from harm and is simply protesting about this change in sleeping arrangements. You do *not* want to put your baby through five minutes of crying to then send them mixed signals and undermine the program.

In my opinion, it's more damaging to prolong a program because you are doing it half-heartedly (and it takes much longer to achieve) than teaching baby the right way for a few nights.

Now, prepare yourself for the exact same routine for the rest of the night. The first time your baby wakes up, I want you to wait for ten minutes. Then knock slowly and loudly on the nursery door, or shush, for 30 seconds to one minute. Baby should drop the volume of their cry and move to a stop-start grizzle. If your baby is still standing after the first ten minutes, go in (by now it will be dark in the room). Do not make eye contact or talk and lie baby back down in reverse star position, tucking the base of their sleeping bag into the bottom of the cot (and cover them with a blanket if it's cold).

Continue on in ten minute intervals for the rest of this first night. If your baby is quiet in under ten minutes and moves to a stop-start grizzle, put your clock back and start the ten minute wait period again. There may be a window of self-settling during this time so it's important to allow for it and give your baby a chance to self-settle.

Having said all of that, most babies don't start to self-settle on the program until the early-morning hours of night two. So stay on track during this first night. You must expect, in order for baby to get the best learning done, that it will be a busy night.

My preference would be that one of you does that first night while the other gets some rest. Then the rested person can take over in the morning while the other rests.

If your baby hasn't gone to sleep after 30 to 45 minutes and you are feeling distressed or overwhelmed, go into the nursery, pick baby up and take them outside into, say, the lounge (just make sure the lighting is dim) and give them a loving cuddle for a few minutes. You'll feel reassured your because baby will immediately stop crying and you'll see that your precious bundle is totally fine and is simply protesting the change in routine! Now . . . *do not* revert to old habits! Don't offer dummies or a breastfeed or whatever sleep prop your child is addicted to. Just give them a cuddle and, after a few minutes, place them back in the cot, and keep going with the program.

The next day

Both you and your baby will be feeling tired today, and maybe a little fragile. That's OK. You've had a big night of learning, and baby has started to adjust to a new, healthy sleeping routine. So lie low today. Don't plan to do lots of activities that will make baby even more tired or overstimulated. Have a quiet day at home and watch your baby for tired cues and get them into bed for their nap ahead of time.

What about day sleeps?

The moment you see your baby showing signs of tiredness, get them in for their nap. You definitely don't want baby to become overtired. In terms of routine, day sleeps are the same. Place your bub in their sleeping bag in the reverse star position then leave the room, waiting for ten minutes and then doing a loud knock or shush from the nursery door for one minute.

Your baby will cry when your knock or shushing stops, but their cry will drop back each time until they self-settle. The truth is that days are hit-and-miss for the first few weeks after a sleep program.

I tend to treat daytime sleeps as negotiable, but but not the nights. I firmly believe that you will never lock daytime sleeps in until the night sleep is locked in.

So with that in mind let's stick to one rule with the daytime sleeps. As long as your baby is going down independently in the reverse star position then you are on track. If they wake after less than an hour, you can try a re-settle from the door. If, after two attempts at the five-minute wait, knock and re-settle, baby is still crying, get them up. You don't want them crying a lot in the day given that at night you are not in a position to pick them up.

The second night

The second night of the program should be similar to the first, but I would expect less crying and a quicker response from your baby. You should not need to go into the room so much because baby will be beginning to learn to position themselves and to self-settle. Having said that, please don't be despondent if that is not the case. Don't second-guess the program. Your baby can do this. Remember that I have worked with thousands of babies over the years and I can say that—assuming your baby is healthy—your baby is not the first one who cannot sleep through the night.

Don't make the mistake of suddenly blaming teething or hunger for your baby's wakefulness. Remember it is nearly always behavioural and usually a sleep association as to how they settle.

This second night is about slightly extending the time frame of listening to your baby's cry. Trust me, on the second night the cry is not as distressing. So on the second night, try a progressive wait before you knock. Try for a ten- to fifteen-minute wait. If your baby doesn't move to self-settle or start a stop-start grizzle, then do the knock or shush for 30 seconds to one minute. You ultimately want to phase out the knock to help promote self-settling.

The third night

In my experience, 70 per cent of babies are well and truly going down to bed calmer by the third night and most are sleeping through if not self-settling. You are on the home stretch!

Remember that this program is *not* about teaching your baby to sleep through the night without waking at all (though that does usually happen). It's about your baby learning how to self-settle so that if they do wake up during the night, they will be able to get themselves back to sleep.

If your baby is still waking up distressed, repeat the instructions for the second night. After all, every baby and family is different. Your baby will get there in their own time.

My program runs for three nights, but some babies will take five nights. But trust me, babies respond beautifully as long as you, the parent, stay calm, committed and consistent.

As I've said before, it is always distressing to hear your little one cry, but keep reminding yourself that your baby is safe and well and that their cry is simply one of protest. In my opinion, it's simply not fair to make a child dependent on you or a prop in order to sleep. What happens if they have to spend a night away from you? Your child needs to be able to sleep without totally relying on your presence.

So stay strong. Remind yourself that what you're doing is giving your child a lifelong gift of being a great sleeper.

The Gift of Sleep program for

children aged eighteen months

to five years

This program with an older child (in a big-girl or big-boy bed) can take anywhere from ten days to two weeks to lock in. In my experience, this age group is by far the worst affected with disrupted sleep. It really affects their daytime behaviour and extends to their eating patterns, how they behave towards other children at playgroup, sharing, learning and anxiety separation. It's all greatly increased in this age group when they are not getting enough sleep and are fragile because of it.

Have faith. If you stick at it and stay consistent, you will get results.

This program is specifically for children who are in big-girl or big-boy beds and who are not sleeping in a cot.

This program tends to be more about dealing with behavioural issues and takes longer to lock in, but it's equally as important and is as successful as the other two age-group programs.

When I say 'behavioural issues' I'm not talking about naughty behaviour, but about behaviour that your little one associates with going to sleep. When it comes to this age group, parents have issues with co-sleeping, their child running out of bed and into their room or playing lots of games before they eventually decide to crash at 9.30 p.m. And then of course the child may be waking frequently during the night (and coming in to their parents' room again).

What you need for this program to work

What I'd like you to do is buy a toddler gate for your child's bedroom door. It's really important that your child sees that there has been a shift—a visual shift—in how they now go to bed.

Most children are out of sleeping bags at this age and are in beds with side rails for protection. It's also now safe at this age to use a doona, blankets and a pillow.

Step 1

Implement a bedtime routine (see p. 59). Allow your child to choose their own two stories for you to read to them.

Step 2

Place your toddler in bed, cover them up and snuggle them in with their sleep friend (their favourite cuddle toy) and leave the room. Tell them, 'It's sleep time now. Shhh, shhh.' Now leave the room for ten minutes. Your child will most likely be up and crying.

Step 3

After ten minutes, go back into the room and take your child back to bed. Leave the room and again wait ten minutes. Then try doing a loud knock from a wall or a door ten times. This helps provide a sudden distraction and should lower the child's cry. Now it's just a matter of continuing in this manner for the evening.

You don't want to be going into your child's bedroom constantly. Instead, do the wait and knock. Eventually, your child will know they have to go back to bed by themselves. If you keep going into their room, it will become an exhausting game for three nights.

Note

It's really important that you realise these programs are not like magic wands. Older children can be tougher to teach because of behavioural habits and issues. There are no shortcuts. (Trust me, if there were I'd know them!) Instead, if you stay consistent and strong in the first two nights with your beautiful headstrong toddler, you will see the magic results at the end of it.

Twins

If you have twins, I recommend you follow the same program for these babies as the ones explained in Chapter 5 and just follow the steps for the age group your twins fall into. The one change you need to make is that it's extremely important the babies are separated—just for a few nights. Some people like to do separate programs (so they teach each twin at separate times) but I think you get much better results if your babies are taught on the same nights, but in different rooms. This way, they will be moving into the same routine at the same time. It may be a little more tiring initially, but the end result will be worth it. Bring them back into the same room again by the end of the second week. It's also important they are not together when learning so they don't disturb each other during that busy first night. It would be a shame to get one baby finally settled, only for their twin to wake them up. Argh!

Premature babies

I tend to insist parents get clearance from their paediatrician before they start a sleep program for a baby who was premature—particularly if the baby is in the six to nine-month age group. You want to make sure that eliminating a night-feed is the right thing to do for these little ones. Before I start any sleep program, I like to see that the baby is around the 8-kilogram mark. There are exceptions to this rule, but, generally speaking, I think they are faster learners and in turn are faster at settling at this size. Having said all that, we need your baby to have good neck control and good gross motor skills so it's best to wait until they are six months corrected—rather than their delivery date.

Chapter 6

Frequently asked questions

In the following pages you will find answers to the most common questions I get from parents. If your question isn't listed here, please feel free to go to www.thegiftofsleep.com.au where you can ask me questions yourself . . .

FAQs for babies

Q. What if my baby vomits while I am teaching them the Gift of Sleep?

A. This can be distressing for everybody and in my experience it's best to have fresh sheets and a clean sleeping bag on standby, ready to go. Calmly go in and get baby out of the cot. If you have a partner, this could be a good time for them to come in and change your baby's sleeping bag and freshen baby up while you quickly change the sheets and wipe down the cot bars with a little disinfectant so that the smell of vomit does not linger when baby goes back to bed.

After you've cleaned up, you have to put baby back down, as difficult as that is. Do not go back to any dummies, rocking or patting because you feel upset about the baby vomiting. Stay calm and committed. Baby will move back into learning mode once you have left the room. Go back to your wait and knock routine. Whatever you do, don't cave in. If you feel, however, that your baby is genuinely sick and needs medical attention then clearly you should abandon the program at this point and do what is best for your baby.

Q. Do I need to give up the dummy completely or can I still use it when my baby is awake during the day? (Can I use it in coffee shops to keep my baby quiet?!)

A. No! There is no point in working hard on a sleep program and getting rid of sleep props only to then jeopardise all your hard work during the day! It's a slippery slope when you let a child have a dummy during the day and then it's inadvertently left in while the baby nods off. It means you are sending your baby mixed signals. Often it's well-meaning carers, nannies, grandparents or daycare workers who are the culprits! Start as you mean to continue. So at the start of the program, chuck away all those sleep props—except your boobs! And remember that dummies can also affect speech development down the track.

Q. Should I be changing my baby's nappy during the night?

A. No, this isn't necessary unless your baby has done a poo. Babies actually don't wake during the night from having a damp or wet nappy. If you are using cheaper nappies that's great! But try to put baby in the most absorbent nappy you can at night, as they really do lock the moisture in for the duration of the night (roughly twelve hours). And of course if your baby is sleeping you should never wake them to change their nappy. In the unlikely event your bub does a poo (and this usually happens in the early-morning hours) go in when they have woken for their re-settle, and change the nappy (preferably in the cot if possible so as not to overstimulate them). Don't worry about getting every spot of poo. Just take the bulk away and put baby in a fresh nappy. In a few hours they'll be up for the day and you can give them a thorough clean then.

Q. Do some babies take longer than three nights to learn the Gift of Sleep?

A. That depends on a few things, such as the age of the child, and how strictly the parents stick to the program and whether they send mixed messages. No matter how long it takes the key is not to think the program doesn't work. It does. Don't go back to old habits and start second-guessing the program. Don't undo all the brilliant work you've already put in. Remember, your baby is little and, as with anything new in a little person's life, they will take their own time to lock it in. As long as you are following the right method, you're on track to have your baby learning how to self-settle, which in turn means sleeping through the night.

Q. Help! My baby is still standing up in their cot after the first three nights!

A. OK, you could try putting your baby into the reverse star position (on their tummy) and then placing your hands gently on their back to stop them from scrambling straight up. Soothe them *temporarily* in this new position—just until they relax. However this is a band-aid solution—you really just want to do this while your mobile baby grows confident and is weaned off whatever person or prop they previously used to get to sleep. If after three nights standing up is still an issue, my opinion is that it's best not to go in, as your baby is capable of moving back down and lowering into reverse star position themselves. Experience tells me that if you continue to hop in and out of the room, it can be distressing for everyone.

Q. My baby is not 100 per cent healthy but I'm desperate. Should I start the program anyway?

A. No. It's very important that baby is well and that none of the night waking is associated with any illness. In fact, some families like to swing by their GP a few days before they start the program just to be sure that baby is 100 per cent well. Your baby will not learn to self-soothe if they're sick. After all, when a baby is sick they need their parents. It's not the time to learn something new.

Q. Can my partner also do the re-settling?

A. For the first week I think one person (the person who usually puts baby to bed and gets up to them in the night) should be responsible for the teaching. However, after the program is locked in, it's totally fine to transfer the bed routine to the other parent. But in the initial period, continuity in carer is very important. The partner who gets to sleep(!) can take over duties the next day while the other catches up on sleep.

Q. Should I send my toddler to their grandparents' house to avoid the noise disruption from the baby?

A. This is probably one of the most frequently asked questions! Heaven knows, we don't want two poor sleepers by having a crying baby disrupt the toddler. But I can say, with over a thousand programs under my belt, I am yet to have a toddler wake up (unless they were already a very light sleeper). Most toddlers are deep sleepers and do not need the added stress of moving environments.

Q. What do I tell my family and other well-meaning friends?

A. Tell them nothing or everything! Remember that you are setting aside three nights in your life to get this right because you, as a family, have decided it's right for you. Not for your

111

best friend or your mother-in-law or your mum, but for YOU. You don't need to justify your decision to anyone. Most parents who have experienced severe sleep deprivation understand that it's a very lonely place to be at 3 a.m. with a baby not sleeping, and that the ripple effect on your family dynamics can be detrimental. If family or friends are particularly negative, make sure you don't surround yourself with them during the period of the program. Negative energy is draining and you will already be emotional. Surround yourself with people who are supportive and helpful.

Q. Will my baby be fragile the next day or not love me?

A. This is such an emotional question and totally understandable. Trust me, your little baby may be a bit fragile during the sleep program. That isn't from being in sleep school, but more from the disrupted night and volume of sleep while they learn something completely new to them. Remember, you are struggling as a family and this is the right option for you and your family. I assure you that your baby will still be their loving, happy self when you collect them from the cot after the first night You will be proud of them and of yourself for staying consistent. And, after a week, you'll have a happily sleeping child!

Also remember that the results of the Murdoch Childrens Research Institute study into controlled crying said, 'Parents can also feel reassured they are not harming their babies by using sleep interventions.'

Q. How do I listen to my baby's cry and know when to knock or when the baby is actually in distress and I need to intervene?

A. Believe me, after the first couple of hours you will know the different levels of cry your baby has. You'll become an expert at knowing when they are moving to re-settle. The rule of thumb is if they are moving back to that stop-start grizzle then lie low. No knock. No shushing. No going in. If you think after five minutes that is not happening then move to the next step, which is usually a loud knock or shush from the door for 30 seconds to one minute. Remember to secretly check that your baby is lying down in the appropriate star position.

Continue doing the five-minute wait followed by 30 seconds to one minute of knocking or shushing. However, if baby's cry has escalated in pitch and volume, go into the nursery to do a re-settle. This is really to reassure baby that you are with them on this journey.

Having said all of the above, it's important to stress that I am obviously not in the room with you. So at all times use your sensible, safe judgement. If you are concerned something is wrong then definitely check on your baby and be sure.

Q. My baby shares a room with our toddler. When can we bring them back together?

A. I generally say two weeks. It won't take two weeks for baby to be sleeping through but remember your baby is learning to self-settle and, for the first week or so, that will be grizzle-stop-start after the initial program.

Q. Do some babies just never learn to sleep through the night?

A. In my twenty years of experience, no. Not if parents stay consistent, committed and calm. It's rare for the program to not work on healthy, thriving babies.

Q. We live in a really warm climate and so we need to have the fan on in the nursery during the night. How do we ensure our baby doesn't become reliant on the noise of the fan to get to sleep?

A. It's totally fine to have the fan on initially when your baby is put to bed, but once they are asleep and the temperature has dropped, turn the fan off. This will help stop baby relying on it as a prop throughout the night.

Q. If my baby is teething, how do I know that is what is making them wake up during the night?

A. The truth is, teething rarely causes babies discomfort—so don't convince yourself that your child's bad sleeping pattern is because of teeth coming through. If in doubt, you could consider giving your baby some Panadol for children. And, of course, if they have any other unwell symptoms—a temperature or unexplained crying for long periods of time—then see a doctor and definitely put off doing the program until baby is 100 per cent well.

Q. What if I have twins or my baby is premature?

A. There are many programs I have done over the years with disabled older children and special-needs kids and these have still worked well. But the two areas which seem to be becoming more prevalent are twins (of which I happen to be one!) and premature babies.

Please see pages 100 and 101 for more information on adapting the program for these children.

Q. What if I have a reflux baby?

A. Increasingly, families are ringing me to say they are struggling because of having a baby with reflux. Reflux babies do tend to need more manual re-settling, which can in turn lead to poor sleep habits. What you need to remember is that most medical professionals agree that by six months most babies are over the worst of their reflux, so if they're waking repeatedly it could be out of habit rather than from reflux. The solution: definitely consult your GP before you begin a sleep program with any baby who has had reflux. My advice is to remove elevation from the cot. Most reflux babies have considerable elevation (like phone books or stumps under legs of beds, etc.) so best to move them back into a flat position. Certainly give the baby the reflux medication they need as per usual and start the program on a day when they have eaten well and are calm. Reflux babies tend to really benefit from sleeping through as they have had a tougher journey already than most babies. Now it's time to teach them to sleep through, which they are perfectly capable of doing.

Q. How long do I leave my baby doing the stop-start cry?

A. Some babies seem to be able to do a stop-start grizzle for a loooong time! If it has gone on longer than half an hour and it is bothering you, you can go in and gently wake baby fully (as they are often half asleep when they do it). That could mean gently picking baby up and placing them down again with the sheet firmly placed across their chest or back (depending on their age). You could even put them at the other end of the cot. Doing a re-settle like this will lead to a louder cry from your baby initially but you can then guide them back to self-settling with shushing or knocking. Having said that, many families are happy to lie low and leave baby to quietly grizzle. But if it is bothering you, feel free to go in and re-settle baby.

Q. I was going fine on the Gift of Sleep program but now I think my baby is waking because they are teething . . .

A. It's important to use your own sensible judgement as a parent, but I will say that teething does not usually make babies wake in the night unless they are molar teeth. However, if in doubt use Panadol for children or baby-teeth gel so that if baby does wake, you are reassured that you have addressed the pain.

It's also worth putting a barrier cream on baby's bottom during this time as their urine tends to be more acidic when teething and this can lead to nasty nappy rash. It's important particularly during those first few weeks of the Gift of Sleep program to stay consistent and not send mixed signals. Of course, if you genuinely believe your baby is in pain, pick them up immediately, have Panadol or gel ready to give them, cuddle them and then put them back into the start position to self-settle. Holding baby in your arms or feeding them back to sleep will not correct teething!

Q. My baby has been doing well for months, but has started waking in the night so I fed them back to sleep. Is that bad?

A. I think the Golden Rule applies here: if your baby wakes during the night after you've done the Gift of Sleep program and baby is well, then they need to self-settle. If baby is struggling to get back to sleep, by all means go to the door and knock or shush.

Babies are little and, as with anything else in life, they will have their moments but it's important to stay consistent. Try to avoid travelling in the first month after the Gift of Sleep program. If baby comes off track because of sickness, don't worry. Just get back on track and start over, even if it means you have to bring out the sheet again. Many families still take a sheet and a sleep friend with them when they travel. They may not need to put the sheet across baby's chest or back as per the program, but it is a great prompt for baby if needed.

Q. When do I stop tucking in the sheet?

A. By week four you can start to release the sheet from one side for day naps only. If all goes well, then after two or three days take the sheet off fully for day sleeps. Do the same then for nights. Release one side for a few nights, then if that goes well take the sheet away completely for night-time sleeps.

Q. My baby is sick. Do I keep doing the Gift of Sleep program or can I feed or cuddle them to sleep?

A. I have already addressed this in the book, but it is worth recapping.

Rule One: when you are doing the Gift of Sleep program (including in the three weeks after it) try as much as you can to avoid friends and family who are sick. While you are trying to lock in the program, the last thing you want is for your baby to get sick and to have to start over. (I realise that with older kids being at kindy or childcare it's not always possible to avoid getting sick, but certainly do what you can to avoid seeing friends or family who have colds, etc.)

If baby does get sick it does not mean you should fall into old habits of using dummies or feeding or patting baby throughout the night.

If baby wakes, you might wait a few minutes to see if they re-settle—it's your call and depends on how sick they are. If they don't settle, then pick them up and cuddle them in a chair in their room. You may want to give them Panadol for children (or medication the doctor has prescribed). Then put baby back to bed, and continue this during the night. Babies will at most need reassurance and maybe a sippy cup of water then back to bad.

Many people say they feel they should have their baby in bed with them. I'm not a fan of this but in rare cases or if you are worried I favour a mattress close by outside the nursery door or in the corner of baby's room out of sight. This period when baby is sick with a cold usually only lasts two or three nights. Once you see your baby is back to their usual self (e.g. eating well and happy with no fever) then you will know they are well and moving back to calmer night-time sleeps. If baby does wake in the night once they are well again, you may like to go back to knocking or shushing from the door. You could even reintroduce the sheet if you need to. But you should find that once your baby has learned the Gift of Sleep and can self-settle, they will easily go back to self-settling again.

Q. Can we do the Gift of Sleep program if baby sleeps in our room?

A. If baby sleeps in your room that's totally fine, but I would think about having you and your partner (if you have one) sleeping out in the lounge room just for the three nights of the Gift of Sleep program. This will help baby learn how to self-settle alone, without having a parent in the room with them. Then after the first few nights, you can move back in!

Q. If we are travelling with our baby and all sleeping in the same room, will that ruin the Gift of Sleep training we have done?

A. My experience is that most families do not need to go to the expense of getting separate rooms when travelling. We had three little boys in a two-bedroom flat in Sydney for many, many years. (That's right! Three kids in the one room!) You work with what you have in life and there are many families in one-bedroom flats doing the Gift of Sleep program. So when you're away, my tip is to position the cot as far away from your bed in the hotel room as you can. Let baby go off to sleep first with you lying low until they have gone off to sleep. Limit noise. If there is a wake in the night, let baby grizzle and self-settle. If it goes on, stay in bed to limit movement and tap or scratch the bed head for 30 seconds to give bub the cue to go back to sleep. Works a treat every time!

As for the travel cot, I recommend families spend $10 and go to Clark Rubber and get them to cut a piece of foam to size. Place that under the base. This will make the uncomfortable travel cot base seem more like your baby's cot at home.

Q. Our baby found night one of the Gift of Sleep program easy but they are struggling on the other nights. Is that a bad sign?

A. This can happen. Night one for some families is a dream and then baby seems to really protest on nights two, three or four. It doesn't mean the program is not working, or that you are doing something wrong! Your baby is normal and is just taking their own journey to the Gift of Sleep. Just remember the three Cs: calm, committed and consistent.

Q. Ever since we started the Gift of Sleep program, our day sleeps have been harder.

A. My rule is that days will come together after the nights are locked in. However, if during first week of the program, you find it really challenging that baby is not sleeping well during the day, I am totally happy with you giving them a mobile sleep in the car or in a pram in the afternoon. That's not to say they have mobile sleeps all day, because you still want them to learn to self-settle during the day. But here's an example of how a day might work: put baby down in the star position for their morning nap and then give them a mobile sleep for the afternoon. If in the morning, baby wakes after 45 minutes aim to re-settle them by doing the knock or shush or scratch of a pillow to get them back to sleep.

Days are important but I don't want you getting bogged down with them. Nights are not negotiable from day one, but day sleeps are a little more flexible. By that I mean that if baby doesn't want to sleep for longer than 45 minutes and you have tried to re-settle them and it hasn't worked, just get them up.

Q. For some reason the knock and shush seems to make my baby more agitated! What do I do?

A. My thoughts are that the protest your baby is making is not about the knock or shush, but is instead because they are weaning off a sleep prop and are frustrated at not having someone or something to put them back to sleep. Try to stay consistent with the shushing—at the very least it tells baby they are not alone. But if you really feel the knock or the shush sound is not working for your baby, try a different noise. (I list a few on p. 158.) Click a pen. Scratch your nails on a pillow. It will be trial and error but please remember these noises are not to manually put baby off to sleep. Rather they are designed to distract baby during their protest cry. It helps calm them down and move them into sleep mode.

FAQs for toddlers

Q. What if my child takes off their clothes?

A. You don't need me to tell you this is an attention-seeking behaviour! Go in, place the top or nappy (or whatever has been removed) back on your child and put them back into bed. Don't talk or make it a fun interaction. And don't fall into the trap of negotiations!

Q. What if my child keeps asking for water?

A. Again, this is an attention-seeking delay tactic! Kids are smart! Don't fall into the trap of negotiations. Make sure they are well hydrated before they go to bed—and, of course, that they have gone to the toilet before bedtime.

Q. What if my child says they need to go to the toilet?

A. Going to the toilet should be part of your child's 'going to bed' routine. If your little one suddenly claims they need to go to the toilet, give them the benefit of the doubt. Take them to the toilet—once—but make sure no discussions take place. You want the experience to be as dull as possible. Once they have been to the toilet, it's straight back to bed.

Q. What if my child throws their sleep toy away?

A. We are not playing the yoyo game! Re-settle your child and give them back the toy, but don't fall into a game of your little one throwing down their toy and you going in to fetch it. Be firm and tell them that if they throw the toy away again you won't retrieve it for them.

Q. What if my child insists on sleeping with the bedroom light on?

A. This is very common but, really, bedroom lighting needs to be dim. The main light needs to be off or it becomes a stimulus as they watch and can see shadows, which is disruptive to sleep. Night lights and hall lights can be used to help your child get used to sleeping in the dark.

Chapter 7

Dos and don'ts for the next 30 days

You've followed the program and your baby has now learned to self-settle—yippee!—but I believe it takes 30 days to really lock the program in. So, with that in mind, please stick to the following things.

1 **Be strong and stick to the program.** Don't be tempted to take any shortcuts and go back to old sleep props. You've put in the hard work—don't undo everything now by sending your baby mixed messages.

2 **Don't be tempted to suddenly teach your baby anything else right now.** For example, now is not the time to start toilet-training or to move baby out of the cot and into a big bed! Let them have 30 days as a buffer zone to focus on this one task of learning how to put themselves to sleep.

3 **Don't get any vaccinations done this month** (unless they are due and you forgot). It's better to do the Gift of Sleep program when your baby has had all their major injections and has none planned for the month following.

4 **Do this program when you know you have a month at home.** Don't suddenly go on holiday or move house. While your baby is locking in the program, you want to keep disruption to a minimum.

Chapter 8

Case studies

Felix: The six-month-old baby who woke throughout the night for his dummy

The problem: Megan and David's six-month-old son, Felix, went off to sleep easily at night—so long as he had his dummy. The problem was that, every time the dummy fell out of Felix's mouth during the night, he cried until his parents re-plugged it. When she called me, Megan was getting up at least six times every night.

The solution: This is such a classic problem, which so many parents face. What starts out as a lifesaver to keep a baby quiet turns into a prop that they need in order to get to sleep. The three-day Gift of Sleep program worked well on Felix. He wasn't happy on the first night without his dummy, but by the third night he was on that golden journey of self-settling. Short-term angst for long-term gain.

Rowan: The twelve-month-old who stood in her cot and refused to sleep unless she was rocked to sleep in her mum's arms

The problem: Eloise's daughter Rowan had never been a good sleeper and had recently started standing in her cot, and screaming at both day and night sleep times, unless Eloise rocked her to sleep in her arms (and then somehow managed to transition Rowan back to the cot without waking her).

The solution: One thing was clear with Rowan—the rocking to sleep had to stop! This was all about teaching Rowan that she could get off to sleep by herself and didn't need Eloise's rocking arms to do it. It was certainly a challenging situation—for both Rowan and Eloise, who were both attached to the process of Rowan being rocked to sleep—but by the sixth night Eloise had succeeded and Rowan's bedtime tears had stopped. Eloise managed to stay focused and consistent, and within a week Rowan was like a different child, going to sleep independently.

Joshua: The eighteen-month-old toddler who loved to climb out of the cot

The problem: Joshua had recently discovered that he could climb out of his cot. So this once great sleeper would now quite happily climb out of the cot and come out to the lounge every night. His parents, Peter and Terri, weren't sure how to keep him in bed.

The solution: Peter and Terri realised that Joshua needed to be transferred to a big-boy bed but they weren't sure how to keep him in it. First, we did the transfer to the big bed. Initially, we kept the cot up for a few days and let Joshua nap in the big bed during the day and he slept in the cot at night. On the fifth day, his dad took the cot out of his room and Joshua did all his daytime and night-time sleeps in his big-boy bed. That's when we also put a baby gate in the door, which served as a visual cue to Joshua that he wouldn't be able to get out of the room.

Millie: The thirteen-month-old party animal

The problem: Toddler Millie needed everything to get to sleep. Dummies. Rocking. White noise playing in her room. And she still wound up in her parents' bed sleeping with them from 3 a.m. every morning. Mum and Dad were exhausted and Millie was overtired and irritable from lack of sleep.

The solution: One word springs to mind with Millie: overstimulated! With so many sleep props (rocking, dummies, music), Millie was being sent mixed signals. Of course, I understand how this happens. Parents get desperate and try anything to get their baby to sleep so that they end up with a long routine of props they feel their baby needs. Millie was weaned off all of her sleep props and learned how to successfully self-settle. Rest assured that babies like her don't find it harder to do the sleep program just because they have more sleep props to be weaned off. It's all the same.

Harper: The seven-month-old who was hungry all night

The problem: Jane rang to talk to me about her beautiful baby girl Harper, who was reaching all her milestones except for sleeping through the night. She was still being fed to sleep, and Jane realised that Harper was using her breasts as human dummies. If they were not there to suck (even for just a few minutes) whenever she woke, she would not settle. Jane was exhausted, and felt guilty and also slightly resentful of her seven-month-old being so physically dependent on her.

The solution: The key in a situation like this is to make sure your baby is on three meals a day before starting the sleep program. That way you'll know that wakes in the night are not hunger-related! Remember that at six months of age, your baby is fine to have three feeds a day (plus three meals a day) and then sleep for twelve hours at night.

Jane was committed to continuing breastfeeding in the day, but not at night. So we began a program after the evening feed, placing Harper in the cot wide awake and then teaching her over a few nights to wean off the breast and move back to self-settling. Not only did Harper sleep through the night, but she woke up in the mornings with an appetite since she was not now snacking at night.

Jack: The ten-month-old who suddenly needed to be patted to sleep

The problem: Tom and Sharon rang me in desperation. Their son Jack had been an outstanding sleeper but had got sick and fallen into the pattern of needing his dad, Tom, to stay in the room. They had accepted this while he was sick but the pattern soon became permanent and Jack had lost his confidence and forgotten how to get himself to sleep.

The solution: We slowly moved Tom out of Jack's room and allowed Tom to talk to Jack from behind the door, which wasn't closed. There should be no fear at all attached to this process. Tom spoke firmly but lovingly to Jack saying, 'It's sleep time now, Jack.' Followed by 'Shhhhhhhh.' This continued every ten minutes until Jack was calm and quiet.

This is a very common problem particularly for families whose babies have been good settlers but because of illness or travel have fallen into some bad habits.

Willis: The nine-month-old early bird

The problem: Willis was a very good sleeper—he went to bed easily and was able to self-settle during the night. The problem was that he was a very early riser. He wanted to start the day at 4.30 a.m.!

The solution: Teaching a baby to self-settle at 4.30 a.m. rather than start the day at that time can be really challenging. After all, the sounds of the day have often begun: birds are tweeting, garbage trucks are on the move, and sunlight may be streaming through the windows. I got Willis's parents, Deanna and Paul, to refer back to the Gift of Sleep program and move to having a sheet tucked tightly around Willis (see page 64). This sent the message that the day wouldn't start quite yet. Even if it takes a little while, your baby will get the message and eventually fall back to sleep.

Chapter 9

How to not need this book with your next child

From the first day home from hospital with a beautiful new baby, I think all parents should be placing newborns to sleep on their back in their own cot or bassinet. This is in line with SIDS (sudden infant death syndrome or cot death) guidelines. Preferably, the cot or bassinet should be in a quiet area of the parents' room or in baby's own bedroom. These are the first important environmental supports that I believe lead to good sleep habits. Make sure you have a safety-approved bassinet or cot and a firm mattress that fits snugly against all sides of the cot. If you have elected to keep baby out of your bedroom so they will be sleeping in their own nursery from the first night, I recommend you have a baby monitor.

The three most important environmental factors that help a baby to sleep are quiet, dark and warmth. I think it's important to promote these as soon as you come home from hospital—not when baby is four months old and heading for sleep school! The longer a poor sleep pattern goes on, the more entrenched and sometimes difficult it is to break.

It's very important that parents learn to let babies (even newborns) settle themselves sometimes. Try not to run to baby the second you hear them squeak. It's a bit like helicopter parenting! Instead, do a little progressive wait of, say, one to two minutes before you respond. I truly believe this is a major factor as to why families are struggling with sleep routines from six months of age. Allowing your baby to fall asleep in your arms, while being fed (breast or bottle) or with a dummy in their mouth, is making them feel that they *need* these things to go to sleep.

Keeping your baby or child up late does NOT mean a child will sleep later or through the night. Instead what it does is simply rob the child of crucial sleep time. You, in turn, will have an overstimulated, overtired, grizzly baby on your hands the next day.

A great calming influence in my experience is moving bath time to early evening from about three months old. A bath manages to fill the time during that difficult early-evening period when most families struggle with supper-time. For baby, evening can be a bit stressful because so much is happening: older children are coming home, one parent or both may be returning from work, there could be a change in environment from daycare or kindy to home. This can all make baby feel fatigued and stressed. So a nice warm bath followed by a light massage on the change table is a great tool to stick with. Now is not time for one parent to come home and have a big play with baby. We want to keep things quiet and calm.

Be warned! By the time your baby is six to eight weeks old, if you have been using any type of sleep prop (dummy, patting, rocking, driving around the block in the car) now is the time to ask, 'Is this a friend or foe?' If your baby is dependent on these things to sleep or settle, then I say chuck it.

It's all about avoiding sleeping crutches, such as sleeping with your baby so that they will go to sleep. Of course, you can still have that beautiful cuddle time with your baby, but if they fall asleep on you, make sure you wake them before placing them back in the cot.

Before your baby arrives, I would advise that you make decisions early on with your partner about co-sleeping. You need to remember that you may be making a rod for your own back.

Always remember that what may look like the answer to getting baby to sleep in the early days may actually end up turning baby into a very poor sleeper.

From five months onwards, give baby a sleep friend (a special sleeping toy). Sleep blankets are also fine. Whatever you give your baby, just make sure it is safe and free of ties, buttons and ribbons.

From five months on, establish a set bedtime routine for baby every night. (See an example of a bedtime routine on page 59).

The bedtime routine sends a signal to your baby that now it's time for their big night-time sleep, which is different to their daytime naps.

From early on in baby's life, really listen to their cries and try to distinguish between a hunger cry and an overtired cry. Most families fall into the trap of feeding baby when in actual fact they have woken in the night because they have not learned to self-settle.

Keep a behavioural chart (you can download one for free from www.thegiftofsleep.com.au). This is extremely useful in those first twelve weeks of baby's life, which most families will agree is a fairly hit-and-miss time! Once you can rule out hunger and distress, you can teach baby to self-settle. Record your baby's awake time, their crying time and their quiet time. You will slowly be able to watch baby learn to self-settle without having to send them to sleep school!

Sleep is important. If you have this for your baby, everything else will fall into place. Find one or two tricks that work for you and stick with them. If it makes life calmer and more settled for your baby, and if your baby is happy and healthy and sleeping in a way that works well for your family, then that is all that is important.

In the end, you know what's best for you and your baby. Trust your gut instinct. Do what works for you.

The Gift of Sleep

Reference guide

Contents of the reference guide

How much sleep do babies need?   150

Basic routines

Routine for babies aged six to eight months   151

Routine for babies aged nine to twelve months   152

Routine for babies aged twelve to eighteen months   153

Meal ideas for babies aged nine to eighteen months   154

Tips for bed-hopping toddlers   155

Troubleshooting   157

How much sleep do babies need?

Age	Approx. amount of sleep needed per 24-hour period
newborn	16–18 hours
3 weeks	15–18 hours
6 weeks	15–16 hours
4 months	9–12 hours at night plus 2 daytime naps (2–3 hours in total, e.g. 2 x 90-min nap, or 1 x 60-min nap and 1 x 2-hour nap)
6 months	10–11 hours at night plus 2 daytime naps (2–3 hours in total)
9 months	10–12 hours at night plus 2 daytime naps (1–2 hours each)
1 year	10–11 hours at night plus 1–2 daytime naps (1–2 hours)
18 months	10–12 hours at night plus 1 daytime nap (1–2 hours)
2 years	11–12 hours at night plus 1 daytime nap (1–2 hours)
3 years	10–11 hours at night plus a possible daytime nap (1–2 hours)

As the table shows, the amount of sleep needed in the first three years of life decreases over time, for both the night and day. Of course, it's important to say that the amount of sleep needed varies individually from baby to baby. The above is a rough guide.

Basic routines

Routine for babies aged 6 to 8 months	
6.00 a.m.	Breast or bottle feed (180 ml to 240 ml)
6.30 a.m.	Short playtime
7.30 a.m.	Breakfast (mixed cereal, fruit and yoghurt, or toast fingers)
9.00 a.m.	Breast or bottle feed
9.15 a.m.	Settle and sleep
11.00 a.m.	Water and playtime
12.00 p.m.	Lunch (pasta or rice and vegetables, cottage cheese and fruit, or a little cheese stick with grated fruit like apple)
12.30 p.m.	Breast or bottle feed
1.00 p.m. to 3.00 p.m.	Settle and sleep
3.30 p.m.	Water or diluted juice and playtime
5.00 p.m.	Dinner (meat casserole with mashed vegetables, plus custard and fruit)
6.00 p.m.	Bath time
6.30 p.m.	Breast or bottle feed then start bedtime routine
7.00 p.m.	Bedtime

Routine for babies aged 9 to 12 months	
6.30 a.m.	Breast or bottle feed and a play
8.00 a.m.	Breakfast (e.g. mixed cereal, Weet-Bix or rice cereal, fruit and yoghurt, toast fingers)
9.30 a.m. to 11.00 a.m.	Settle and sleep
11.00 a.m.	Water and playtime
12.00 p.m.	Lunch (pasta or rice with vegetables, cottage cheese and fruit, or pieces of soft raw fruit or cheese sticks)
12.30 p.m.	Breast or bottle feed
1.00 p.m. to 3.30 p.m.	Settle and sleep
3.30 p.m.	Water and a playtime or a walk
5.00 p.m. to 5.30 p.m.	Dinner (e.g. chopped chicken or fish casserole, or patties with mashed vegetables, plus custard and fruit)
5.45 p.m.	Soothing bath and a baby massage on the change table
6.00 p.m.	Breast or bottle feed
6.30 p.m. to 7.00 p.m.	Bedtime

Routine for babies aged 12 to 18 months

6.00 a.m. to 8.00 a.m.	Breast or bottle feed, and breakfast, brush teeth, quick wash and get dressed, then play about the house.
9.00 a.m.	Morning tea
10.00 a.m. to 11.30 a.m.	Off to the shops, the park, or playgroup (a great opportunity to learn about playing together and sharing)
12.00 p.m.	Lunch at home with a sippy cup of water or milk
12.30 p.m.	By now baby should be exhausted, so a quick nappy change and off to bed
3.30 p.m.	Wake up and have afternoon tea
4.00 p.m.	Playtime around the house or a trip to the shops or park
5.30 p.m.	Toddler dinner (no later or baby will be too tired)
6.00 p.m.	Bath and get dressed for bed
6.30 p.m. to 7.00 p.m.	Breast or bottle feed and bedtime routine

Meal ideas for babies aged nine to eighteen months

Breakfast

- Baby muesli.
- Porridge and yoghurt.
- Finger food.
- Pieces of fruit and toast.
- Avocado on toast. Cottage cheese on toast.

Morning and afternoon tea

- Finger food like pieces of peeled raw fruit.
- Dry biscuit with avocado or cheese spread.
- Cheese sticks.
- Drink of water in a cup.

Lunch

- Baked beans.
- Avocado and cheese sandwiches.
- Scrambled egg or vegetable omelet.
- Macaroni cheese or spaghetti.
- Chunky vegetable soup with toast.
- Stewed fruit and yoghurt or custard.
- Pieces of peeled raw fruit.

Dinner

- Beef casserole and veggies.
- Pasta or rice with veggies.
- Lentils and veggies.
- Fish patties with rice balls.
- Steamed vegetable pieces.
- Rice pudding with fruit jelly.

Tips for bed-hopping toddlers

*(Children aged eighteen months to five
years who are sleeping in big beds)*

- When it comes to sleep issues with older kids, it is behavioural (but not naughty behaviour).

- **When moving your child into a big bed make their room and the new bed as inviting as possible.** Let them choose their new doona cover or sheets and pillow. You can get a character they love like Dora or Spiderman to make it seem exciting and fun. You want your child to absolutely love their room and to love spending time there. Moving into a big bed can be a celebration of becoming a big boy or a big girl, and they get to be in a big bed!

- Make sure the bed is not too big. I'm not a big fan of king singles because I think they can be too big and little kids can feel lost in them, particularly after coming from a cot.

- Establish a bedtime routine, exactly as you would with little ones who are in a cot. Bedtime should be something your child looks forward to—sitting in a cosy chair having one-on-one time with Mum or Dad, having a story, saying a prayer, singing a favourite song softly together, talking about what you did that day . . . and then a kiss and a cuddle when they're in bed.

- Make sure your toddler goes to the toilet and brushes their teeth just before bed. Limit drinks an hour before bed, where possible. This will discourage your child from playing games that they suddenly need to go to the toilet.

- For a bed-hopping toddler, put a baby gate up at the door. The first time your toddler gets up out of bed and goes to the gate, tell them 'It's sleep time now' and lead them back to bed. After that, if they get up, don't talk, just lead them back to bed and tuck them back in. Make the experience as boring as possible. Continue on at ten-minute intervals.

- Another strategy is, if your toddler keeps standing at the baby gate calling for you or crying, tell them you will come in and give them a cuddle if they get back into bed first. This encourages them to put themselves back to bed before you come in. Then do a progressive wait with each time you go back in (so, wait an extra minute or two before you head back in).

- Create a sticker chart for staying in bed. For example, if they can stay in their own bed all night for five nights in a row, they get a toy or a great experience.

- Do not lie down in bed with your child. If they are sensitive about you leaving the room, it will just send mixed signals to them and make it harder to leave.

- Be firm but fair. Establish that your child needs to sleep in their own beautiful bed and make no exceptions. Don't weaken and give in to grizzling and whining. Stay calm, committed and consistent.

- Even if you are exhausted or it's an ungodly hour and your child appears at the gate or worse at the side of your bed, get up and don't overreact. Don't be angry. Don't give the whole thing too much attention; simply say gently that it's time to go back to bed and lead them back.

Troubleshooting

My baby is still crying . . .

If after a considerable time—say twenty minutes—you can honestly say your baby's cry is not lowering and you are both emotionally fragile, then you can try moving baby up the bed to a part that is cool and dry and try again. They can often be calmer if they can feel the coolness of the sheet.

Another trick—but not one to be used regularly—is to get baby up and calm them down in your arms. Don't go back to feeding or dummies or any other old tricks to calm them down; just calm them in your arms for three to five minutes. The majority of bubs stop crying immediately. You will be reassured that they are OK and they will be happy to get a cuddle. After a few minutes, place baby back down and continue with the program. Baby may then give a few more minutes of protest crying, and then silence.

If, after 30 minutes or so, your baby is still unhappy and you are unhappy, you can lie on the floor of their room out of sight and gently shush or scratch a pillow softly with your nails. If your baby has a really strong attachment to a sleep prop (like a dummy) this can be a good strategy. Please don't think the program is not working, or that your baby is the one in a million who can't do the program—no, no, no! They are just taking a little longer, as they may have a stronger dependency on their sleep prop than other babies.

If the knocking or shushing sound seems to annoy your baby, then move to another noise that will distract and interest them— like a pen clicking (do it from the floor, out of sight), or clicking your tongue from outside the door loudly, or scratching your nails on a pillow or on the carpet. This might sound silly but it works! Babies become interested in the sound and forget to cry!

My baby's day sleeps have gone haywire!

Remember to put your baby to bed the Gift of Sleep way during the day. If they wake after 30 minutes, that's disappointing but welcome to sleep school! It can take up to a month to lock in daytime sleeps. Try for one re-settle. Check baby is tucked in with the sheet, then leave the room and shush from the door (I wouldn't do the knock at this stage as baby is usually only grizzling not doing a loud cry). If you're still having no luck, give baby a mobile sleep in the afternoon—so, let them have a sleep in the pram or in the car. I'm a bit more open to negotiation with day sleeps, in the sense that I am happy for you to get baby up if you are having no luck after one re-settle. But with night-time sleeps you need to stay firm!

My baby has started waking up between 4 a.m. and 5 a.m. and wants to start the day! HELP!

Some people find their babies start waking between 4 a.m. and 5 a.m. wanting to start the day! The problem is, this makes for a very long day for you and baby—and if you're in a daylight-saving region, well a 4 a.m. wake could quickly become 3 a.m.! Ouch! So you want to make sure baby learns to re-settle.

The key to conquering this is to manually wake your baby before they would usually wake. (So if they have been waking at 5 a.m., go in and wake them up at 4.30 a.m.). Gently pick baby up and make sure they wake up (most bubs will wake quickly as at that time of the morning they are moving into lighter sleep). You just want to make sure baby is awake. Put them on your shoulder and wait until they do a little grizzle. Then place them at the opposite end of the cot and put them back to bed exactly the same way: sleeping bag tucked under the base, and sheet across their back or chest. Now do a normal re-settle—wait outside the room for ten minutes to see if baby drifts back off to sleep. If they are still grizzling after ten minutes shush or scratch on a pillow. (Don't do the knock at this time of the morning.)

You want baby to learn how to self-settle in the early morning before it becomes light and the day starts. (Check that baby's room is still nice and dark—they may be waking because light is coming in). I think if baby locks in sleeping from 6.30 p.m. until 5.30 a.m. that is a negotiable start to the day. But you wouldn't want baby starting their day any earlier than 5.30 a.m. Always try to leave bub in bed for ten minutes or so in case there is a window of opportunity that they self-settle.

STILL HAVING ISSUES?

Remember that I am available to do phone consultations if you feel you need extra support or have further questions. You can contact me directly through my website: www.thegiftofsleep.com.au

Testimonials

Lindsay, Dean and Mila

At six-months-old Mila was waking up every two to three hours—I couldn't settle her without feeding. As a result, I was exhausted in the mornings and didn't have any energy for my very active three-year-old son. I wanted to give him attention but was always irritable and tired due to interrupted sleep with the baby at night.

Essentially Mila went down at 7 p.m., was up again at 9 p.m. and had a feed. Then she slept till 11 p.m. or midnight. Then she was up again at 3 a.m. and then again at 5 a.m. She was wide-awake at 5 a.m. so I had to get up with her. I did attempt to re-settle her before feeding but didn't want to let her cry because I was afraid she would wake my son.

Elizabeth taught Mila how to self-settle. We are definitely happy that we went through a sleep program as Mila now sleeps from 7 p.m. until 5 a.m. or 5.30 a.m. Although Mila still wakes earlier than we would like, we are ecstatic that she can sleep through the night without waking.

It is extremely important to stick to the three Cs: to be calm, consistent and committed to the program. This will ensure that your baby really learns and can easily self-settle.

Gaye, Pete and twins Gwen and Max

Elizabeth came to my husband and me through a referral within our network. She had conducted sleep programs for a number of our friends and everyone was raving about this woman with the magic wand.

We had just been blessed with twins (our first newborns) and my husband and I were struggling to find a balance between their needs and ours as a couple. The reason: a lack of sleep!

We met Elizabeth and from the moment of introduction, my husband, the twins and I felt a genuine connection—upon reflection, quite extraordinary really.

Elizabeth so empathetically understood the desired outcomes we wanted to achieve, pacified our concerns that we were doing something wrong, mapped out a definitive plan (sleep program) then delivered on it.

The results were immediate and the behavioural changes across both twins from a sleep perspective were profound—as in within the next 24 hours! And most importantly for us, it has remained sustainable.

As first-time parents we also took advantage of her email support and follow-up sessions. It has been wonderful to know Elizabeth is available to support us in the very specific issues relating to our family. If you are challenged with a similar issue (lack of sleep due to your baby's immediate needs), STOP NOW, search NO further. Elizabeth is the one.

Sophie, Chris and baby Willow

Our daughter Willow was the most planned, welcomed and loved addition to our family. In fact when I had her I remember telling my closest friends and family that I experienced the most overwhelming sensation of love when she came into our lives, and I meant it with every fibre of my being. I know Chris (my partner) felt the same.

Initially we experienced some issues when we brought Willow home. I couldn't feed her and she was losing weight. She wasn't sleeping but we thought nothing of it.

Once we had her on a bottle she slipped into a good routine, sleeping through from about ten weeks. I even remember being fairly smug about it, making such cavalier statements as, 'I could have another baby tomorrow!' But then we encountered the house of cards that was Willow's allergy, reflux and subsequent sleeping issues.

At four and a half months things started going pear-shaped. She was waking constantly and was always very upset. We took advice from everyone: doctors, friends, family, Google . . . but we were greeted with, 'That's what babies do. Get used to it.'

We continued on, every night getting worse than the one before. The more we researched, the more we were led to believe that babies with reflux weren't able to be sleep trained. We believed this to an extent as we had tried some controlled crying (out of sheer desperation) and it ended in severe vomiting after only three minutes.

The nights were getting worse. At first Willow was waking three times a night, then every two hours, then every hour, then multiple times an hour. As for day sleeps, well, they were non-existent. In the end we had tried projectors, dummies, and an hour-long night-time routine (which we stuck to feverishly), co-sleeping, pram sleeping, couch sleeping. We worked out that we were averaging four hours or less of broken sleep a night. It was affecting our work performance, our social lives and our relationship but most importantly it wasn't allowing us to enjoy Willow as completely because we were all so damn tired.

I finally managed to get Willow's allergy under some control and as soon as this happened (at ten months) I called Elizabeth. I had read about her on the internet and seen an interview with Mia Freedman and I knew she was the one to ask for help.

When I first contacted Elizabeth, I must have sounded fairly frantic! To be honest, I was so tired I barely made any sense! But from our first conversation she reassured me. I felt I could breathe again. Elizabeth, like us, didn't like controlled crying, was sympathetic to our situation and was ready to help.

The first night both Chris and I were nervous, feeling like we were relinquishing our parental duties but exhausted enough to leap forward nonetheless.

Elizabeth began by getting to know Willow, slowly, gently. Then the circus tent came down. By that I mean the palaver we had established to try to aid Willow's sleep was stopped. Next were Elizabeth's techniques. Willow resisted with a full-scale vomit at first but gradually over the next three nights calmed and by the third night had started on the road to normal sleeping.

Now, I must be honest, sleeping through didn't happen straight away (it took a month), although the improvements were immediate. There was some work for us but with Elizabeth's support and advice we were able to persevere. We would never have been able to start or continue the process without her

One month later, Willow was sleeping through the night (although was still a shockingly early riser!) and was even having two naps a day. Is Elizabeth a miracle worker? ABSOLUTELY!

John, Rebecca and Evie

When Elizabeth came to us I was feeling completely fed up! As Evie was our second child I probably had less energy or even, dare I say it, sympathy for being woken up at night. I was cranky, sleep-deprived and not enjoying life at all. I didn't feel like myself at all—I felt like I couldn't be a good mother to my first child or even Evie as I was just existing through the day rather than getting up and embracing it and enjoying my children and my life. And there were a couple of times I was cranky with the children and of course felt pretty terrible about that.

At nine months old Evie wasn't too bad—waking up just twice a night. But as she got older she was taking longer and longer to get back to sleep (through breastfeeding), so often I would be up for an hour at a time at least. Her first wake-up was around 10 p.m. or 11 p.m. so there wasn't much sleeping time left in the night for me. Ugh. Bad memories!

I felt like a new woman after Elizabeth came. And Evie was a much happier baby too! Of course I was nervous and unsure as to how it would work and whether it would work, but it completely changed our lives. The fact that we were all sleeping well at night completely changed our family dynamic (no more cranky Mum!) and I felt like I could return to my normal self and normal life. I felt like me again. The biggest testament to Elizabeth's techniques was when Evie got sick two days after the program (Elizabeth saying that the worst thing that could happen would be that Evie would get sick during the program . . . and lo and behold!). But even then, Evie still slept well at night with no wake-ups. I was pretty amazed and surprised to be honest, and it made me realise how powerful the sleep program is. I'm so glad we did it.

The best thing for me is the confidence I have that whatever has happened in the day I know that when I put Evie down to sleep at night she will stay asleep until the morning (unless she is sick) and wake up a happy and refreshed baby. You have no idea how relaxing that thought is for me. And even though we've had illnesses and overseas travels since the program, Evie gets back on track quickly and easily which again I see as testament to how effective the program is and continues to be.

Charlotte, Matt and Oliver

We were up every two to three hours for Oliver. I was still feeding at 3.30 a.m. Six months had passed and we were all very tired, including bubba. Tears were flowing! No one was really functioning at their best during the day.

Oliver was a good sleeper during the day but all of sudden it came to a head and he became restless night and day. He became addicted to the dummy! I was up every few hours popping it back in. He was going down at about 7 p.m. and would ALWAYS wake about an hour afterwards. We'd have to throw down our dinner before he woke so one of us could hold him until he went to sleep again. We had eeeeeverything to try to make him sleep: a singing lamb, patting, warm milk, tip-toeing around the house. Crazy!

Before Elizabeth came, I was also still doing a 3.30 a.m. feed. My husband works an early shift and it meant we were ALL exhausted by the afternoon.

Implementing Elizabeth's Gift of Sleep program was the best thing we ever did. I was recommended to go through with it by a dear friend who is a great mum. She told me it was going to be a tough three days and it was. In fact, it was still tough a few weeks afterwards. Every so often, I'd have to do some controlled crying on my own. But a few months on and we didn't hear from Oliver at all. He's now almost two years old and never, ever wakes in the night. Sometimes I hear him stir and he goes back to sleep in a flash! My husband calls it the best investment we ever made. Our nights are full of sleep. Our days are full of action. And, best of all, our baby flourished and we have no doubt that's because he has slept well. Elizabeth saved us!

Steve, Gabriella, William and Xavier

We were exhausted and I felt like I wasn't functioning properly in daily life. Everything seemed to require so much effort. My head was permanently foggy. Steve was spending a lot of nights sleeping in the spare bedroom as he had to get up and go to work and William, who was six months old, was in a bassinet in our room.

William was waking three to four times during the night. I would breastfeed him to get him back to sleep every time. During the day I would also have to feed him to sleep. He had no self-settling ability whatsoever and zero routine in terms of bedtime. I was also still wrapping him.

The second time round with Xavier I had learned from some of my past mistakes so things weren't as bad, however by five and a half months he was still waking once or twice a night and I was getting up to feed him.

Elizabeth completely turned our lives around. From the first night she came into our home there were no more night feeds. My boys could both suddenly go twelve hours straight without a feed! William learned how to self-settle. I could now place him in the cot awake and unwrapped and walk out of the room without him letting out a single cry! It was a miracle. He became a poster child for sleeping—both in the days and the nights. Within days he developed a huge appetite for solids, which until then he hadn't been overly interested in.

I felt as though I gained hours of time back to myself during the day that I had previously spent trying to get him to fall asleep, and that's obviously not to mention the whole family finally getting a good night's sleep for the first time in over six months. Having Elizabeth come and do a sleep program was one of the best things we have ever done and worth every cent. The sleepless nights were so much easier to get through with our second son, as we knew Elizabeth was the light at the end of the tunnel.

We still follow all the sleep guidelines that Elizabeth taught us. Our toddler is an excellent sleeper and is happy to go to bed every night. As a first-time mother I learned so many things from Elizabeth, and not just in regards to sleep. She also provided me with a framework for how to structure the baby's day.

Michael, Tania and baby Eva

Before Elizabeth arrived I was feeling very anxious about my baby Eva, who was six months old, not being in a good sleeping pattern. The whole house felt chaotic and stressed. It all felt overwhelming and scary. I couldn't function with the lack of sleep. I also felt guilty for being so cranky and moody and emotional to my two other kids and husband.

We had a witching hour from about 6 p.m. to 9 p.m. where Eva would not settle and thus affected her next sleep cycle. And, of course, she was very restless. I couldn't relax or spend time with my husband when he returned from work, or be with my other kids.

Essentially, Eva would wake every three hours and I found it very hard to stretch her further.

Elizabeth walked in the door at 9 p.m., took Eva and worked her magic. Eva responded immediately to the sound of Elizabeth's voice and her touch as if she was saying 'thank you' to Elizabeth for coming and giving her the gift of sleep. Elizabeth was able to immediately settle Eva and put her down to sleep for a good four-hour stretch. This became longer and longer until she was almost going through the night.

When Elizabeth was in the home I felt an instant calmness. She was another mother to my daughter—someone who we could trust with our precious baby. One hundred per cent.

The program has been a real success with all three of my children. We were able to resume an almost normal life (with sleep!) within no time. There are no words to say thank you!

Jonny, Louise and Sonny

Sonny had never been a great sleeper from birth. We'd spend hours walking him in the pram while he screamed the neighbourhood down. He used to sleep for as little as twenty minutes sometimes. If he hit the magic 40-minute mark we were over the moon. He was awake for what seemed like the whole night sometimes. Night blended into day without us getting a wink of sleep. It was pretty horrific.

We read every book going on the subject and tried every technique but nothing seemed to work. It appeared we were blessed with a beautiful baby boy who was full of energy and bags of personality but was unfortunately allergic to sleep! It didn't help that all the other mums and dads we knew had perfect little snooze machines. This only added to the frustration.

It was all a bit of a fog at the time. We struggled and it caused big moments of tension and stress between Mum and Dad. We were angry, sad and bloody tired! We were at our wits' end as we tried to battle through it all. Life was happening all around us, as we got more and more tired. It was pretty heart-wrenching to hear your first-born scream so much at night, for him to be so tired and for us to be so helpless. When both of us were back at work that became even harder. Sleep deprivation is so debilitating and it felt like it would never end.

We used to run Sonny ragged all day in the hope of tiring him out for a good night's sleep. We had a routine in place before bedtime. Bath time, milk, into his sleeping bag, dropping him into his cot, then wafting a blanket over him before we used to leave. He screamed straight away. We put an extractor fan on as white noise. Sometimes he would then go off to sleep for a while but he was pretty much up and down. We tried controlled crying, tag-teaming the responsibility throughout the night, holding his hand for hours but he would wake up the moment we let go. We used to whisper downstairs for fear of waking him up and watch the television with our noses 6 inches from the screen. More often than not one of us would end up in the spare bed with him, eventually falling asleep from exhaustion. When he did wake up in the morning he was always overtired and miserable. This went on for two years!

We were expecting another baby and had reached breaking point so Elizabeth was our last resort. To be honest we were sceptical at first about how effective Elizabeth could possibly be, but she came into our lives like an angel from heaven. She sorted Sonny out in three tough days. He started sleeping eleven to twelve hours straight! We were blown away and we haven't looked back. Sonny sometimes wakes in the night but will self-settle and go back to sleep. We don't have to tiptoe around the place. We all sleep and Sonny wakes up in great form in the morning. We're all happy. Life is normal.

We can't thank Elizabeth enough. She has a very special gift. She gave us confidence, some proper ground rules but most importantly happiness.

Worksheets

Checklist

- ☐ Toys other than sleep friend, bumpers, pillows removed from cot
- ☐ Mobile removed from cot
- ☐ Cot positioned away from direct light
- ☐ Cot positioned so it is able to be viewed from the doorway
- ☐ Clean sheets and sleeping bag ready in case of accidents during the night
- ☐ Mattress protector (if it has a plastic backing) removed from cot
- ☐ Cot base lowered
- ☐ All sleep props (dummies, music, etc.) taken out of the nursery!
- ☐ Toddler gate installed (if applicable)

Bedtime routine

Make a note here of what you will do as your bedtime routine for baby so you can do the same thing each night

_____

_____

_____

_____

_____

_____

_____

_____

_____

Knock, wait and re-settle

On the following page, make a note of when you knock or shush, when baby cries, and the length of time they cry for each time. Under 'Cry Type' indicate whether baby is doing a S/S (stop-start cry) or rate the cry's intensity from 1 to 10 (1 being a slight grizzle and 10 being a distressed wail). Any cry you would rate as a 7 or more indicates you should go in to re-settle your baby.

Day One

Time	Cry type	Mon	Tue	Wed	Thur	Fri	Sat	Sun
5.00 a.m.								
5.30 a.m.								
6.00 a.m.								
6.30 a.m.								
7.00 a.m.								
7.30 a.m.								
8.00 a.m.								
8.30 a.m.								
9.00 a.m.								
9.30 a.m.								
10.00 a.m.								
10.30 a.m.								
11.00 a.m.								
11.30 a.m.								
12.00 p.m.								
12.30 p.m.								
1.00 p.m.								
1.30 p.m.								
2.00 p.m.								
2.30 p.m.								
3.00 p.m.								
3.30 p.m.								
4.00 p.m.								
4.30 p.m.								

Day One *continued*

Time	Cry type	Mon	Tue	Wed	Thur	Fri	Sat	Sun
5.00 p.m.								
5.30 p.m.								
6.00 p.m.								
6.30 p.m.								
7.00 p.m.								
7.30 p.m.								
8.00 p.m.								
8.30 p.m.								
9.00 p.m.								
9.30 p.m.								
10.00 p.m.								
10.30 p.m.								
11.00 p.m.								
11.30 p.m.								
12.00 p.m.								
12.30 am								
1.00 a.m.								
1.30 a.m.								
2.00 a.m.								
2.30 a.m.								
3.00 a.m.								
3.30 a.m.								
4.00 a.m.								
4.30 a.m.								

Day Two

Time	Cry type	Mon	Tue	Wed	Thur	Fri	Sat	Sun
5.00 a.m.								
5.30 a.m.								
6.00 a.m.								
6.30 a.m.								
7.00 a.m.								
7.30 a.m.								
8.00 a.m.								
8.30 a.m.								
9.00 a.m.								
9.30 a.m.								
10.00 a.m.								
10.30 a.m.								
11.00 a.m.								
11.30 a.m.								
12.00 p.m.								
12.30 p.m.								
1.00 p.m.								
1.30 p.m.								
2.00 p.m.								
2.30 p.m.								
3.00 p.m.								
3.30 p.m.								
4.00 p.m.								
4.30 p.m.								

Day Two *continued*

Time	Cry type	Mon	Tue	Wed	Thur	Fri	Sat	Sun
5.00 p.m.								
5.30 p.m.								
6.00 p.m.								
6.30 p.m.								
7.00 p.m.								
7.30 p.m.								
8.00 p.m.								
8.30 p.m.								
9.00 p.m.								
9.30 p.m.								
10.00 p.m.								
10.30 p.m.								
11.00 p.m.								
11.30 p.m.								
12.00 p.m.								
12.30 a.m.								
1.00 a.m.								
1.30 a.m.								
2.00 a.m.								
2.30 a.m.								
3.00 a.m.								
3.30 a.m.								
4.00 a.m.								
4.30 a.m.								

Day Three

Time	Cry type	Mon	Tue	Wed	Thur	Fri	Sat	Sun
5.00 a.m.								
5.30 a.m.								
6.00 a.m.								
6.30 a.m.								
7.00 a.m.								
7.30 a.m.								
8.00 a.m.								
8.30 a.m.								
9.00 a.m.								
9.30 a.m.								
10.00 a.m.								
10.30 a.m.								
11.00 a.m.								
11.30 a.m.								
12.00 p.m.								
12.30 p.m.								
1.00 p.m.								
1.30 p.m.								
2.00 p.m.								
2.30 p.m.								
3.00 p.m.								
3.30 p.m.								
4.00 p.m.								
4.30 p.m.								

Day Three *continued*

Time	Cry type	Mon	Tue	Wed	Thur	Fri	Sat	Sun
5.00 p.m.								
5.30 p.m.								
6.00 p.m.								
6.30 p.m.								
7.00 p.m.								
7.30 p.m.								
8.00 p.m.								
8.30 p.m.								
9.00 p.m.								
9.30 p.m.								
10.00 p.m.								
10.30 p.m.								
11.00 p.m.								
11.30 p.m.								
12.00 p.m.								
12.30 a.m.								
1.00 a.m.								
1.30 a.m.								
2.00 a.m.								
2.30 a.m.								
3.00 a.m.								
3.30 a.m.								
4.00 a.m.								
4.30 a.m.								

Day Four

Time	Cry type	Mon	Tue	Wed	Thur	Fri	Sat	Sun
5.00 a.m.								
5.30 a.m.								
6.00 a.m.								
6.30 a.m.								
7.00 a.m.								
7.30 a.m.								
8.00 a.m.								
8.30 a.m.								
9.00 a.m.								
9.30 a.m.								
10.00 a.m.								
10.30 a.m.								
11.00 a.m.								
11.30 a.m.								
12.00 p.m.								
12.30 p.m.								
1.00 p.m.								
1.30 p.m.								
2.00 p.m.								
2.30 p.m.								
3.00 p.m.								
3.30 p.m.								
4.00 p.m.								
4.30 p.m.								

Day Four *continued*

Time	Cry type	Mon	Tue	Wed	Thur	Fri	Sat	Sun
5.00 p.m.								
5.30 p.m.								
6.00 p.m.								
6.30 p.m.								
7.00 p.m.								
7.30 p.m.								
8.00 p.m.								
8.30 p.m.								
9.00 p.m.								
9.30 p.m.								
10.00 p.m.								
10.30 p.m.								
11.00 p.m.								
11.30 p.m.								
12.00 p.m.								
12.30 a.m.								
1.00 a.m.								
1.30 a.m.								
2.00 a.m.								
2.30 a.m.								
3.00 a.m.								
3.30 a.m.								
4.00 a.m.								
4.30 a.m.								

Day Five

Time	Cry type	Mon	Tue	Wed	Thur	Fri	Sat	Sun
5.00 a.m.								
5.30 a.m.								
6.00 a.m.								
6.30 a.m.								
7.00 a.m.								
7.30 a.m.								
8.00 a.m.								
8.30 a.m.								
9.00 a.m.								
9.30 a.m.								
10.00 a.m.								
10.30 a.m.								
11.00 a.m.								
11.30 a.m.								
12.00 p.m.								
12.30 p.m.								
1.00 p.m.								
1.30 p.m.								
2.00 p.m.								
2.30 p.m.								
3.00 p.m.								
3.30 p.m.								
4.00 p.m.								
4.30 p.m.								

Day Five *continued*

Time	Cry type	Mon	Tue	Wed	Thur	Fri	Sat	Sun
5.00 p.m.								
5.30 p.m.								
6.00 p.m.								
6.30 p.m.								
7.00 p.m.								
7.30 p.m.								
8.00 p.m.								
8.30 p.m.								
9.00 p.m.								
9.30 p.m.								
10.00 p.m.								
10.30 p.m.								
11.00 p.m.								
11.30 p.m.								
12.00 p.m.								
12.30 a.m.								
1.00 a.m.								
1.30 a.m.								
2.00 a.m.								
2.30 a.m.								
3.00 a.m.								
3.30 a.m.								
4.00 a.m.								
4.30 a.m.								

So now what?

Now you remind yourself that you're not alone on this journey—because you're not.

Please remember that I am available for phone consultations if you feel you need extra support or have further questions. You can arrange this by contacting me directly through my website: www.thegiftofsleep.com.au

And don't forget that you can always contact PANDA (Perinatal Anxiety & Depression Australia) on 1300 726 306 (www.panda.org.au) or BeyondBlue on 1300 22 4636 (www.beyondblue.org.au).

Acknowledgements

I would like to thank the following people.

My family, for allowing me to fly the nest every night to spend time helping other families yet still being there in the morning with love and smiles when I arrive home. You are amazing and I couldn't do what I do without you.

I want to thank Mia for believing in me for so many years, long before this book came together, and for encouraging me to take the step of putting my thoughts down so I could share this program with families everywhere. Mia, it's your love and support which has placed me in a position to be able to share my knowledge and passion. It would never have happened without you.

Thank you to the thousands of families who have allowed me into their homes and trusted me with their precious children. It has been an honour working with each of you.

Elizabeth Sloane

Index

3 Cs *see* three Cs

6- to 8-month-olds
  daytime routine 151
6- to 11-month-olds
  bedtime routine 59
  daytime sleeps 69–70
  Gift of Sleep program
    first night 63–9
    second day 69–70
    second night 71–2
    third night 73–4
  premature babies 101, 115
  sleep requirements 150

9- to 12-month-olds
  daytime routine 152

9- to 18-month-olds
  meal ideas 154–5

12- to 18-month-olds *see also*
  toddlers
  bedtime routine 59, 79
  daytime routine 153
  daytime sleeps 87
  Gift of Sleep program
    first night 79–86
    second day 86–7
    second night 88–9
    third night 90–1

18-month- to 5-year-olds *see
  also* toddlers
  bed-hopping 155–7

18-month- to 5-year-olds
continued
  bedtime routine 95–9
  Gift of Sleep program 93–9

aggression 29, 31, 66, 83
air-conditioners 50, 51
amount of sleep required per
  age 150
anxiety 29, 66, 83
attention difficulties 29, 66,
  83
attention-seeking
  behaviour 123
Australian Association for
  Infant Mental Health 28

baby monitor 141
baby/toddler gate 97, 133,
  156, 157, 156, 181
back, sleeping on 63, 141
bath time 59, 142, 143
bed-hopping toddlers, tips
  for 155–7
bedding
  blankets 49–50, 98
  cot sheets 53
  pillow 52, 98, 181

sleeping bags 51
tucking in 64, 80, 82, 85,
  118, 137, 158, 159
wraps 64
young children 98
bedtime routines 29, 58–9
  6- to 11-month-olds 59
  12- to 18-month-olds 59
  18-month- to 5-year-
    olds 95–9, 124, 156
  checklist 181
  importance of 56, 57–8, 144
  notes 182
  saying goodnight 59, 98,
    156
  story time 58–9, 98
behavioural chart 144
behavioural issues 97, 155
behavioural problems 29, 30,
  31, 66, 83
BeyondBlue 195
blankets 49–50
  cellular 50
breastfeeding 35, 68, 69, 81,
  86, 135, 142, 170, 173

calm 46, 55 *see also* three Cs
car, sleeping in 121, 143, 159

checklist for bedtime 181

clicking *see also* noise

  pen 122, 158

  tongue 158

clothes, toddler taking

  off their 123

cognitive problems in

  babies 29, 30, 31, 66, 83

cold weather (colder

  months) 50

comfort settling 65, 82

committed 43, 46, 55–6 *see*

  also three Cs

consistent 46, 55, 56 *see also*

  three Cs

controlled crying 5, 27, 168

  case against 28

  case for 29–32

  Gift of Sleep program

    and 37–8

  safety 30

  study 29, 30–1, 112

co-sleeping 97, 134, 143, 168

cot

  base 52, 120–1

  bedtime checklist 181

  blankets 49–50

  bumper 52, 181

  climbing out of 133

  mattress 52, 141

  mattress protector 52, 181

  mobiles 53, 181

  pillow 52, 181

  position 51–2, 53, 120, 141,

    181

  safety 52

  sheets 53

  standing up in 77, 80, 84,

    110, 132

  toys 53, 181

  travel 120–1

  tucking baby in 63, 80, 82,

    85, 118, 137, 158, 159

cot death *see* SIDS (sudden

  infant death syndrome)

crying 28, 37, 70, 71, 81, 87

  controlled *see* controlled

    crying

  'cry it out' 32, 37

  duration 116

  escalating 66, 72, 82, 84,

    113, 116

  Gift of Sleep program

    and 43–4

  hunger 144

crying *continued*
  interpretation 13, 65, 82,
    113, 144
  protest 37, 74, 122
  rating 183
  reducing 65, 67, 70, 85, 98
  sleeping position 64
  stop-start 66, 67, 71, 82, 85,
    89, 113, 116
  troubleshooting 157–8
  worksheets 45, 65, 183
cuddling 69, 86, 118, 119,
  143, 156, 158

darkness 141, 160
daytime routine
  6- to 8-month-olds 151
  9- to 12-month-olds 152
  12- to 18-month-olds 153
daytime sleeps 12
  6- to 11-month-olds 69–70
  12- to 18-month-olds 87
  difficulties 121–2
deprivation of sleep 4, 23, 32,
  39, 112, 176
dimmer switch 51–2
dummies 9–10, 27, 36, 39,
  58, 64, 69, 71, 81, 83, 107,

119, 131, 142, 143, 157,
  172
  daytime use 108

early wakers 137, 159–60
exhaustion 4, 68, 84
eye contact 82, 85

fans 50, 114
five-minute knock and
  re-settle *see* knock and
  re-settle
food
  meal ideas for 9- to
    18-month olds 154–5
  solids 36, 135

game playing 97, 98, 123,
  124, 156
gate, baby/toddler 97, 133,
  156, 157, 156, 181
Gift of Sleep program 35
  6- to 11-month-olds 59,
    63–74
  12- to 18-month-olds 59,
    79–91
  18-month- to
    5-year-olds 95–9

case studies 131–7

controlled crying, use
of 37–8

disruption 46, 118, 120–1,
128

dos and don'ts 127–8

duration 37, 44, 74, 91, 109

environmental factors 141

eye-contact 82

five-minute wait, knock and
re-settle *see* knock and
re-settle

goal 38, 73

Golden Rules 43–6

minimum age of baby 28,
29, 30, 36

minimum weight of
baby 36, 101

note-taking 45, 144, 182,
183

nursery preparation 49–54

nutrition 45–6

premature babies 101, 115

reflux 115–16, 167–8

shortcuts 127

siblings, effect on 111,
113–14

suitability assessment 38–9

support 43, 44, 45, 112

taking turns by partners 68,
86, 111

three Cs 46, 55–56, 121

timing 44, 46

tone of voice 65, 66, 81, 83

travelling 36, 45, 118,
120–1, 128, 136

troubleshooting 157–60

twins 100, 115, 166

venue 45

Golden Rules 43–6

health 43, 115 *see also*
sickness

hot weather (warmer
months) 50–1

hunger 71, 88, 135, 144

knock and re-settle 65, 67, 70,
71, 81, 84, 87, 113, 122

lamps 51

learning difficulties 29, 66, 83

light sleepers 36

lighting 51–2, 53, 124, 160
dimmer switch 51–2
hall lights 124

lighting *continued*
    night lights 124
    sleeping with light on 124
massage 59, 143
meal ideas *see also* food
    9- to 18-month-olds 154–5
mobile sleep 159
mobiles 53, 181
monitor, baby 141
Murdoch Childrens Research
    Institute
    infant sleep research 29,
        30–1, 66, 83, 112
music 9, 134, 181 *see also*
    noise

nappy
    night changing 63, 79, 108
    rash 117
neighbours 44
newborns
    self-settling 142
    sleep requirements 150
    sleeping position 141
night feeds 9, 27, 36, 63, 79,
    117–18, 135, 144, 172,
    173
night lights 124

noise 122, 158 *see also* music
    knocking 65, 67, 70, 81, 84,
        87, 98, 107, 113, 122,
        158
    nails on pillow 122, 158
    pen/tongue clicking 122,
        158
    reliance on 51, 114
    sensitivity 53
    white 134, 176
nursery
    baby monitor 141
    bedding 50, 51, 52, 53, 64
    cot *see* cot
    lighting 51–2
    temperature 49–51, 141

overstimulation 31, 53, 69,
    86, 109, 134, 142
overtiredness 12, 70, 87, 134,
    142, 144

PANDA (Perinatal Anxiety
    and Depression
    Australia) 195
partners
    support 45
    taking turns 68, 86, 111

pen clicking 122, 158

postnatal depression 29, 30, 31, 39

pram, sleeping in 35–6, 121, 143, 168, 176

premature babies 101, 115

progressive wait 65, 71, 82, 89, 142, 156

protest cry 37, 74, 122

quiet 141

reflux 115–16, 167–8

REM (rapid eye movement) sleep 36

re-settling 65, 66–7, 82–3, 113, 116, 119

  by partner 111

resources

  agency contacts 195

  telephone consultations 161, 195

reverse star position 79, 82–3, 84, 85, 87, 110

rewards 156

rocking and patting to sleep 9, 27, 35, 39, 83, 107, 119, 132, 136, 143

room-sharing see also bed-hopping; co-sleeping

  parents 120–1

  siblings 113–14

routine 56, 57

  bedtime see bedtime routine

  daytime see daytime routine

safe sleeping guidelines 52, 53, 63, 77, 141

scratching nails on pillow 122, 158, 160

self-settling 65, 71, 73, 109, 119, 121, 134, 144, 159

  alone 120

  crying 70, 87

  early morning 137, 160

  goal 38

  newborns 142

  promoting 64, 72, 80, 89, 116

  skill 22, 35, 88, 90

  time until 85, 90, 131

  tucking in 64

  window of opportunity 66, 67, 82, 85, 160

separation anxiety 31, 95

settling
  comfort settling 65, 82
  re-settling 65, 66–7, 82–3
  self-settling see self-settling
  timing 67, 83
shushing 65–8, 70, 72, 81–9,
  98, 113, 116–22, 136, 158,
  160, 183
sickness 54, 107–8, 110, 115,
  118–19, 136
SIDS (sudden infant death
  syndrome) 52, 53, 63, 77,
  141
sleep friend 53–4, 58, 63, 81,
  98, 118, 124, 143, 181
sleep programs 66, 83
  Gift of Sleep see Gift of
    Sleep program
  minimum age 28, 29, 30,
    36, 83
  minimum weight 36 , 101
sleep props 9, 27, 35, 43, 51,
  58, 69, 74, 81, 83, 86, 91,
  108, 114, 127, 134, 158,
  181
sleeping bags 51, 53, 98
sleeping crutches 143

sleeping position
  back 52, 63, 64, 141
  newborns 141
  reflux 115–16
  reverse star position 79,
    82–3, 84, 85, 87, 110
  star position 64, 67, 70, 113
  tummy sleeping 77, 79–80,
    83, 110
sleeping through the night 6,
  11, 23, 36, 37, 73, 114,
  135, 169
solid food 36, 135
soothing 84, 110
star position 64, 67, 70
  reverse 79, 82, 85, 87, 110
sticker chart 156
story time 58–9, 98, 156
sudden infant death syndrome
  see SIDS
support network 43, 44, 112

teething 71, 88, 114–15, 117
temperature
  colder months 50
  gauges 49
  nursery 49–51, 141
  overheating 52

self-regulation 49

warmer months 50–1

three Cs 46, 55–6, 74, 91,
121, 157, 165 *see also*
calm; committed;
consistent

toddlers *see also* 18-month- to
5-year olds

attention-seeking
behaviour 123

bed-hopping 155–7

big bed, transfer to 133, 155

bedtime routine 95–9, 124,
156

climbing out of cot 133

drinks before bed 156

gate 97, 133, 156, 157, 156,
181

sleep disturbance 111,
113–14

sleeping with light on 124

sticker chart 156

taking clothes off 123

throwing sleep toy 124

toilet after bedtime 124

tongue clicking 158

toys 53, 143, 181 *see also* sleep
friend

travelling 36, 45, 118, 120–1,
128, 136

troubleshooting 157–60

tummy sleeping 79–80, 83,
110

twins 100, 115, 166

vaccinations 37, 46, 127

voice
bedtime farewell 59, 98,
156
shushing *see* shushing
tone 65, 66, 81, 83

vomiting 107–8, 169

white noise 134, 176

witching hour 175

wraps 64

Notes

Notes

Notes

Notes

Notes

_____

_____

_____

_____

_____

_____

_____

_____

_____

_____